Trade Unions
In A Free Society

Trade Unions
In A Free Society

*Studies in the organisation of labour
in Britain and the U.S.A.*

B. C. ROBERTS
Reader in Industrial Relations, University of London

With a Foreword by Professor F. W. Paish

Published for
THE INSTITUTE OF ECONOMIC AFFAIRS
by
HUTCHINSON OF LONDON

HUTCHINSON & CO. (*Publishers*) LTD
178-202 Great Portland Street, London, W.1

London Melbourne Sydney
Auckland Bombay Toronto
Johannesburg New York

★

First edition 1959
Second edition 1962

*This book has been set in Times type
face. It has been printed in Great Britain on
Antique Wove paper by Taylor Garnett
Evans & Co. Ltd, Watford, Herts, and
bound by them*

Contents

FOREWORD   F. W. Paish   9

PART ONE: UNIONS IN BRITAIN

I THE PRINCIPLES AT STAKE   15

II TRADE UNIONS AND WAGE PROBLEMS
The case for a national wages policy – Union bargaining power – Wages and the level of demand – The
lessons of national wages policies – Co-operation for
information – Differentials – Fringe   benefits – Pension
schemes – Profit sharing – Productivity and restrictive
practices   20

III TRADE UNIONS AND INDUSTRIAL RELATIONS
The right to strike – Compulsory arbitration – The
role of the Minister of Labour – Plant grievance arbitration – The conduct of strikes – Shop stewards – Joint
consultation   44

IV TRADE UNIONS AND POLITICS
The role of the T.U.C. – Relations with the Labour
Party – The political levy – The politics of trade union
democracy – The prevention of electoral malpractice –
Apathy   59

V TRADE UNION STRUCTURE AND ORGANISATION
Number and size of unions – Types of union – Closer
unity – Breakaway unions – Freedom of association –
Compulsory unionism – Trade union leadership –Trade
union finance   76

VI SUMMARY OF CONCLUSIONS   93

PART TWO: UNIONS IN THE U.S.A.

                                                       99
I INTRODUCTION

II THE STRUCTURE OF UNION ORGANISATION
The development of union structure – Inter-union
relations – Growth in the power of the AFL-CIO –
Growth in union size   106

CONTENTS

III UNION DEMOCRACY

Control of the executive – Appeals procedure – Self-regulation – The right to choose a union   124

IV CORRUPTION

The setting – The internal fight against corruption – Governmental control – Employer attitudes – Corruption and society – Labour Management Reporting and Disclosure Act, 1959   143

V WAGE BARGAINING AND THE CONTROL OF INFLATION

The problem of creeping inflation – Are the unions responsible for inflation? – The cost of controlling inflation – A national wages policy   157

VI INDUSTRIAL RELATIONS

The climate of industrial relations – The character of industrial strife – Is it in the contract? – Arbitration – Militancy and efficiency – The growth of personnel management – Worker participation – Trade unions and profit sharing – Union control over industrial investment – A national council for Industry   168

VII UNIONS AND POLITICS

The development of political activity – The Democratic Party – Labour and Liberals – Political power – Campaign Funds   185

VIII CONCLUSIONS   196

SHORT BIBLIOGRAPHY   201

INDEX   203

THE AUTHOR

B. C. ROBERTS was born in Leeds in 1917. After working in a variety of occupations he obtained a trade union scholarship to the London School of Economics. From there he won a scholarship to New College, Oxford. Read P.P.E. After graduating was awarded a research scholarship at Nuffield College and a part-time lectureship at Ruskin College, Oxford. In 1949 he was appointed Lecturer in Trade Union Studies at the London School of Economics, and in 1956 appointed Reader in Industrial Relations. Sometime visiting Professor of Industrial Relations at Princeton University and Massachusetts Institute of Technology. Author of five books and many articles. Has travelled widely and lectured all over the world. Consultant to various research projects. Has taken part in many management training programmes in public and private industry. Currently engaged on a study of the development of industrial relations in the tropical areas of the Commonwealth. Frequently broadcasts and appears on television.

Foreword

ONE of the major problems in a changing world is to prevent institutions which have been developed to meet a particular need from surviving, when that need has disappeared and been replaced by others, in a form which hampers further growth. Even where the process of re-adaptation is ultimately achieved, there inevitably intervenes a period of strain and difficulty, when an institution has ceased to perform its original functions but has not yet been sufficiently adapted adequately to perform its new ones. Trade unions throughout the world seem to be going through such a period of strain today. High among their original objectives was the protection and increase of the real incomes of their members; and, so long as their members collectively constituted only a small minority of the employed population, they were often able to achieve their objective. But as the aggregate of their numbers grew, it became increasingly difficult for any one union to achieve exceptional benefits for its own members without at the same time inflicting detriment on the members of other unions.

In this study of trade unions in the United Kingdom and the United States, Mr. Roberts rejects the view that the faster rise in money incomes than in output, which has been so marked a feature of many economies since the war, has been caused by the power of the unions to force up wages. He contends that, with full employment, it is the competition between employers for scarce labour which forces up wages, or which, even if standard wage-rates are pegged, forces up actual earnings. He points, indeed, to some non-unionised occupations where earnings have risen faster than those

9

in which unions are strong. While, however, the blame for the post-war inflations cannot be laid at the door of the unions, Mr. Roberts believes that the effects of their actions may well be to increase the minimum amount of unemployment which is consistent with the absence of inflation.

If the unions are to be exculpated from the charge of being the force behind inflation, they are at the same time debarred from claiming that they have caused the general level of either money or real wages from rising faster than it would have done in their absence. If it is also true that they may increase the minimum amount of unemployment which is consistent with the absence of inflation, they may also find that, as inflation is checked, they have increased the average level of unemployment and slowed down the growth of output. There is therefore a case for believing not only that the unions have ceased to achieve one of the most important of their original objectives, but also that, in pursuing it in changed conditions, they are, in the result, acting to the detriment not only of the community at large, but often, in the long run, of their own members as well.

The problem now is how to induce the unions, in the present changed conditions, to refrain from individually pursuing policies which in fact frustrate their collective objectives. For this problem Mr. Roberts offers no easy and simple solution. In a free society trade unions can be neither prohibited nor made subservient to government policies; only under the most authoritarian regimes can enforcement be ruthless enough to make the laws effective. Nor do the records of attempts to impose compulsory wage structures, maximum wage rates, or even compulsory arbitration offer much encouragement to further experiments in these directions. Compulsory strike ballots are as likely to increase as to decrease the danger of strikes; and mere machinery for joint consultation is of little help without more fundamental changes.

Mr. Roberts's own suggestions are less simple and less spectacular. The government must do its share by providing a non-inflationary economic climate. Bad labour relations are often the result of tactless, secretive, or incompetent management. In the United Kingdom misunderstanding and suspicion would sometimes be avoided by more clearly defined contracts of employment. The unions need larger, better-paid and less over-worked staff. More emphasis should be laid on negotiations at workshop level. Shop stewards should be more closely integrated into the main structures of their unions, and members should be given more information about how their union is run and more protection against possible injustice from it. The problem, in short, must be solved by education and understanding rather than compulsion.

In the United States, where the history, organisation and outlook of the unions are very different from those in Britain, the problems are also different. Here there is no need to ask for better pay for trade union staff, or to suggest more clearly defined contracts. The need is for a better check on the almost unlimited powers of the senior officers of unions, a much greater regard for scrupulousness, or even morality, in their methods, and above all a relaxation of the atmosphere of bitter mutual hostility in which negotiations between employers and unions only too often take place. Here Mr. Roberts puts his main hopes in a gradual amelioration of the general ferocity of American business life and a change in outlook to something nearer that of Britain.

If at the same time the mild tempo of British business life could be injected with some of the competitive urgency of the American, the reduction in the contrast between the two systems would be to the benefit of both.

To the understanding of the difficulties and problems of labour relations and trade unions, both in Britain and in the United States, this book, like Mr. Roberts's earlier writings, makes a notable contribution.

F. W. PAISH

October, 1961.

PART ONE
Unions in Britain

I

The Principles at Stake

(TRADE unions in a free society are an expression of the fundamental right of men and women to organise themselves in order to
protect and promote their interests by collective action) It cannot
be assumed, however, on the basis of the mere existence of trade
unions that a society is democratic, since the ruling oligarchies in
totalitarian societies of both the right and the left have made use
of trade unions to achieve their ends. There are, however, basic
differences in the powers and functions of trade unions under conditions of democracy and dictatorship.

In a free society the right to organise implies the right to exercise
the power that collective action carries within the scope of a liberal
legal framework. A democratic society is, by definition, one in which
power is not concentrated entirely or substantially in the hands of
the government; in modern terms this means that power is diffused
through a multiplicity of agencies. In other words (voluntary
organisations, such as trade unions, have an important role to play;
they should, therefore, enjoy the freedom necessary to exercise their
functions in industry and to exert political pressure on the government to legislate in their favour.)

A totalitarian state, by contrast, does not permit a voluntary
association to exercise rights that might conflict with the policy of
the government; therefore such independent institutions as trade
unions have to be nationalised along with every other form of private enterprise. Making trade unions into an agency of the state
is justified by the argument that the state always acts in the best
interest of the workers, and that it therefore follows logically that
the duty of the unions is to ensure that the state achieves its ends.
The principal function of the unions is not, according to this

15

doctrine, to pursue a policy which their members think is in their own best interest, but to act as a transmission belt between the infallible state and the rank-and-file citizens.

The notion that there is an automatic and continuous identity of interest between those who hold the reins of government and the objectives of any sectional group is accepted in a free society only in so far as all are expected to respect the conventions and obey regulations which establish and protect the rights of all parties. In a free society it is recognised that the interests of different groups will inevitably conflict, and it is of the essence of democracy that these social conflicts shall be settled by an interplay of social and political forces. It follows from the fundamental assumptions that trade unions in a democratic society must be independent of both employers and state. Without independence the freedom to bargain collectively and to exercise the right to exert political pressure is a mirage that vanishes as soon as it is closely approached.

Independence of control by the state or employer does not, of course, mean that the activities of trade unions in a democratic society should be completely unregulated by law. Every association which wields social and economic power, holds property, and enters into contracts with its members must be subject to those laws which such societies have developed to assist their members to resolve their personal and group conflicts. There are, in fact, considerable differences in the legal methods chosen by democratic states to regulate the behaviour of trade unions, and some of the more important provisions adopted by other countries will be referred to in the course of this work. But when these legal restraints are compared with those in force in Britain it can be said with certainty that in no other country in the world are trade unions less restricted by law.

Trade unions have not always enjoyed the degree of freedom from legal restraint which they have today. The Courts did not look upon the organisation of workpeople and growth of collective bargaining with equanimity. To lawyers who were firmly attached to the concepts of personal rights and individual contracts embodied in the English common law, this development ran against the grain. A succession of statutes was required to free the unions from the taint of illegality and to establish the right to organise, to hold property, to strike and to engage in political activities. Gradually the Courts accommodated their opinions to the emergence of collective action and over the past half-century they have reinforced the decisions of the legislators by a succession of decisions.*

The freedom with which British trade unions are able to run their own affairs has been aptly described as *laissez-faire collectivism*,† and the question has been properly put by many writers in the past few years whether it is possible, under modern economic and social conditions, to leave trade unions to enjoy their present degree of autonomy without seriously jeopardising the interests not only of the general public but also of their members. It is alleged that trade unions have now grown so large and powerful and so bureaucratic in their government and administration that they may threaten the very liberties and social welfare they were created to advance.‡

This study seeks to examine the way in which the trade unions exercise their rights and privileges in carrying out their functions. The author starts with the assumption that free trade unionism is an essential feature of a free society, and that, whenever it is possible and consistent with modern needs and equity, it is better to leave issues of social conflict to the autonomous solution of the parties rather than to administrative or legal regulation.

Granting freedom to voluntary organisations to settle by collective bargaining such questions as the level of wages to be paid to their members clearly removes them from the power of the state. The government must instead seek to influence the level of wages indirectly by its general economic policy, by extending its influence as a major employer itself, and by exhortation to all and sundry. It is equally obvious that the state cannot distribute the labour force according to some plan worked out in Whitehall if it permits workpeople to choose their own jobs and trade unions and employers to settle issues affecting employment and remuneration by independent bargaining.

Although the state must have an employment policy, it must seek

* For an account of the evolution of the law see O. Kahn Freund, 'The Legal Framework', in *The System of Industrial Relations in Great Britain*, ed. by A. Flanders and H. A. Clegg; and Sir Henry Slesser, 'The Legal Status of Trade Unions', in *Agenda for a Free Society*, Hutchinson for I.E.A., 1961.

† O. Kahn Freund, *Labour*, a lecture given in the series 'Law and Opinion in the 20th Century' at the London School of Economics and Political Science, 1957-1958.

‡ *A Giant's Strength*, a study made by the Inns of Court Conservative and Unionist Society. See also J. A. Lincoln, 'Human Rights in Industry', in *Agenda for a Free Society*.

to attain its ends by influence and persuasion, by broad economic and social controls, rather than by the specific direction of voluntary organisations or individuals. So long as the policy of the government may be tried, tested and rejected by voluntary associations, the claim may reasonably be made that the state is democratic. From the fact that the state ought not to decide such issues as the level of wages over the heads of the trade unions, it also follows that the state should not become the universal employer. If that were ever to happen, the unions would find themselves deprived of their bargaining strength, and wages would become a political issue to be settled either at the hustings or by the opportunistic promptings of the party in power.

It is difficult to believe that British trade unions really wish to see established an economic and social system that must inevitably strip them of their traditional rights, destroy their independence, and reduce them to impotence. Yet this is what the unions assert they are aiming to achieve. In practice, they are not likely to accept the drastic limitations on their freedom that the achievement of state socialism would entail. That they would resist such encroachments one may be sure, but the intellectual confusion which their present ambiguous attitude involves is the source of much misunderstanding and also of the failure of the unions to play their proper part. If the unions are to make a constructive contribution to the future welfare of the nation they must come to terms with the market economy, which is an essential feature of a free society, and not seek to prevent it from working. Thus, the problem of trade unionism in a free society is one that can be solved only by the unions in co-operation with the employers and the government.

The state has its role to play, but in a free society it must not be allowed to usurp the proper functions of the unions and employers though it must ensure that neither unions nor employers abuse their power at the expense of the public or of their members. The relationships between the state, unions and employers is bound to change over time, but there is no reason why pessimistic conclusions from extreme individualists or the state socialists should be accepted. The former would have unions abolished in order to return to an out-of-date form of society; the latter would sacrifice their independence and integrity in order to establish a totalitarian system of public ownership and centralised state control. Neither experience nor logic suggests that these extremes are inevitable alternatives; there are solid grounds for believing that, given goodwill, tolerance and an appreciation of the issues that are at stake, a *modus vivendi* can be maintained in a social and economic setting that both provides the maximum degree of personal freedom and encourages the optimum degree of public responsibility.

These issues have now been sharpened by the possibility that Britain will enter the Common Market. The movement of labour over the wider area will mean eventually the establishment of a labour market that is less under the control of the unions and the government of any one member country. Unions, employers and the government will be compelled to adjust their ideas and traditional practices to take advantage of the new opportunities for social advance that the Common Market will offer. Whatever changes in attitude and policy may come, it seems clear that the Common Market will have a profound impact on the conduct of trade unions and the welfare and prosperity of their members. But whether we go in or remain outside the Common Market, we live in a time of rapid change and we will be compelled to face the fact that our future standard of living and status in the world depend upon the readiness with which we jettison worn out methods and develop new techniques in their place.

II

Trade Unions and Wage Problems

THERE are few subjects of social significance with which the trade unions do not concern themselves today, but the vast increase in the range of their interests and activities has not diminished their principal responsibility, which is the negotiation of changes in wages and allied working conditions. It is estimated that the wages and working conditions of more than three-quarters of all employees, trade unionists or not, are determined by collective bargaining with employers and the decisions of statutory authorities in which the trade unions participate.

Every industry now has some form of negotiating machinery. This varies from industry to industry, but it may be classified into two main types: voluntary and statutory. The voluntary procedure, which has been established jointly by employers and unions, is the more significant by far in terms of numbers of workpeople covered and the economic importance of the industries concerned. Engineering, coal, railways, steel, textiles, chemicals and building, all have a well-developed machinery through which collective bargaining takes place on a voluntary basis.* By comparison, statutory machinery, namely wages councils, the Agricultural Wages Board and the Catering Wages Boards, cover industries in which, in the main, the units of production are small, trade union organisation is relatively weak, and wages have traditionally been low. The statutory wage-fixing bodies are not so far removed from the process of free collective bargaining as may perhaps be supposed. Although they have an independent chairman and associates, their members do not, as a rule, seek to enforce their ideas upon the representatives of the

* See the Industrial Relations Handbook published by the Stationery Office.

unions and the employers; rather do they seek to secure agreement between the two sides, acting more like conciliators than arbitrators, though in the last resort they have to choose which side to support.*

Whether settled through voluntary or statutory machinery, the matter which is bargained about at the highest level is the basic weekly or hourly wage rate. This rate, when determined by the statutory bodies, is legally binding and only in special circumstances are employers allowed to pay less.† In the majority of industries the basic rate is not legally enforceable, except in so far as it might have been determined by the Industrial Court under the Issues Procedure which permits it to give an award compelling an employer to pay recognised terms, but in the post-war period few employers have dared to cut the rates set by voluntary agreements.

Though collective bargaining at the national level is about changes in the basic wage rate, only a tiny fraction of employees in the manufacturing industries are paid at these rates. The great majority of production workers have, in recent years, taken home in their pay packets perhaps a third or a half as much again. What actually makes up the earnings of an employee is an amount compounded of the basic wages rate, additions for overtime and week-end work, incentive bonus, shift premiums, merit money and other extras that the employer sees fit to pay. These additional elements that go to make up the total pay packet are often the subject of local bargaining at workshop or company level, conducted by shop stewards or union district officials.

Total earnings are, therefore, determined by negotiations at both national and local levels. This situation, which is the result of the empirical development of industrial relations in Britain, has certain advantages, since it permits a degree of flexibility in the determination of actual earnings which is appreciated both by employers and workers. However, under conditions of over-full employment, the considerable element of 'wage drift', which this pragmatic system of bargaining induces, is an important element in the constant tendency of wages to rise at an inflationary rate. The gap between wage rates and earnings, if the demand for labour were to fall, would

* C. W. Guillebaud, *The Wages Councils System in Great Britain*.
† Special permission may be granted by the statutory bodies permitting an employer to pay below the legal minimum in cases of partially disabled persons.

diminish,* but given national bargaining there is always likely to be some spread between the levels of rates and earnings. Even when there is quite considerable unemployment, some labour markets will still be tight; some employers will have full order books and will be anxious to obtain the labour that they require, and if it is scarce, mobility may be induced only by special offers. Experience since September 1957 has also shown that even when demand is cut back to non-inflationary levels there will still be a substantial amount of overtime worked.

The case for a national wages policy

It is suggested by some economists that to prevent wages from rising, under full employment, far more quickly than the total output of goods and services requires a 'national wages policy'. This expression is, in itself, somewhat ambiguous; what is usually meant is either: (1) the establishment of a national body legally empowered to determine wage levels nationally; or (2) a system of national agreements between the T.U.C. and the British Employers' Confederation, supported by supplementary compulsory controls; or (3) some form of compulsory arbitration operating under the aegis of a national arbitration court.

In each case what is being suggested is the centralisation of wage determination in the hands of a small body capable of pursuing a deliberate policy of wage control. This idea has certain attractions since it seems to promise an answer to the wages problem and it appeals strongly to some who dislike the freedom which a market economy confers upon those who have something to sell or buy. It is argued by the critics that the system of free collective bargaining operates like the law of the jungle; economic rationality is perverted, equity is ignored and the biggest and strongest obtain the best reward. The net effect of this unbridled pursuit of sectional interests is that wages in general are pushed up at an inflationary pace and the structure of differentials which emerges is chaotic, economically inefficient, and grossly unfair.

The indictment is bolstered by reference to anomalies, to cases where unskilled porters earn more than skilled craftsmen, to instances of professional men and women earning less than general labourers or machine minders. That such instances of apparent in-

* As it did when unemployment went up to 2·2 per cent in 1958–59.

equity exist there can be no doubt, but in themselves such examples do not constitute a valid case against free collective bargaining. They may well indicate that certain differentials require adjustment and that deliberate steps are necessary to achieve a more desirable relationship. It does not follow, however, that the baby should be thrown out with the bath water: that collective bargaining should be abandoned and replaced by a centralised system of wage determination.

Union bargaining power

It must also be emphasised that it does not follow automatically that, because wages have risen faster than output, inflation has been caused by the pressure exerted by the trade unions. The notion that trade union bargaining strength is entirely independent of the general situation is clearly disproved by the course of economic events. Unions have been able to push wages up to inflationary levels simply because employers have been willing to meet demands for increases at these rates. In other words, the general economic situation has been such that for many years employers have known that they could pass on increases in wage costs to the consumer in the form of higher prices without much fear of losing business. Indeed, the considerable divergence between the levels of nationally negotiated wage rates and the actual amount employers have been willing to pay their employees has indicated that the unions have not by any means squeezed their market opportunities to the maximum.

The suggestion has been made that the unions will abandon demands for excessive wage increases only at the cost of large-scale strikes.* This point of view is based upon the theory that since 1939 there has been a tacit compact between unions, employers and the government, under which the unions, in exchange for the maintenance of economic conditions which allowed them to obtain substantial annual wage increases, refrained from exercising their full industrial strength. Past experience shows that unions generally respond sharply to major changes in economic conditions, and it could be predicted that the slowing-down of inflation would lead to an increase in industrial unrest. Recent history has shown, however, in spite of the long bus strike in 1958, that unions are not as

* H. A. Clegg and Rex Adams, *The Employers' Challenge*, 1957.

insensitive to changes in the economic climate as the authors of the above theory assumed. It was apparent that the economic situation did not permit the payment of wage increases in 1958 of the order of many previous years, and the majority of unions accepted this fact without strike action.

Wages and the level of demand

The evidence points unmistakably to the fact that the rate of wage increase is closely geared to the general level of demand. When this latter is excessive to the point at which job vacancies far exceed the available supply of labour, then it does not require strong trade unions to push wages up. Employers are only too ready to pull wages up to the level that they consider to be necessary to obtain the supply of labour which they require. If further proof of this statement is required it is found in the fact that the wages of domestic servants, who are practically unorganised, and of agricultural workers, who are very weakly organised, rose by more than any other groups during the inflationary period. In contrast, before the war it was quite impossible for the miners to raise their wages significantly, despite one hundred per cent organisation, in the depressed condition of their industry.

It would, therefore, seem to follow that the best way of preventing an inflationary wage-price spiral would be to see that the aggregate level of demand is not allowed to reach the point at which excessive wage increases are inevitably induced. Unfortunately, it is not easy to regulate the level of demand with such skill that too much wages pressure is not created. When obvious signs of inflation appear it is clearly necessary to take some action, otherwise the correction that will ultimately have to be applied will be far more drastic and painful to bear. The problem which has yet to be solved is how, when cutting back the aggregate level of demand by monetary restriction and other more specific measures, to avoid a general setback to the rate of economic growth.

The T.U.C. in its various submissions to the Chancellor of the Exchequer has severely criticised the use of monetary measures, such as a high Bank rate, to curb excessive spending; it has repeatedly suggested that the problem ought to be solved by a policy of expanding productivity rather than contracting demand. It is, of course, obvious that if the rate of economic growth was faster, a higher rate of wage increases could be tolerated, but the crucial question to which the T.U.C. has given no answer is how to achieve the much higher rate of economic growth desired without running into the danger of inflation. When, as in 1960, after a year of spectacular economic growth, the signs of inflation and a balance of payments problem began to occur what was the right policy to pursue? If no steps had been taken to check the excess demand that was rapidly building up to dangerous proportions another bout of substantial price increases and a massive balance of payments crisis could not have been avoided. There may be legitimate differences of opinion as to the most appropriate measures to be applied, but some kind of effective curb has to be used. The only practical alternative to cutting back demand by monetary, fiscal and hire purchase restriction policies, must be to introduce direct controls over incomes such as a national wages policy and dividend limitation. There are quite a number of people who would argue that if the price of checking inflationary wage advances by general economic measures is industrial stagnation, then it is better to maintain a level of economic activity that would stimulate an inflationary rise in wages and to prevent this consequence by a national wages policy.

There are, however, several weaknesses in this seemingly attractive argument. In the first place, the evidence of past rates of economic growth does not indicate that aggregate demand must be maintained at an inflationary level in order to promote a high level of investment and rapidly rising production. It is obvious that the government's restrictive economic policy did check the growth of the economy for a time, but it did not prevent a substantial rise in the rate of investment in such vitally important areas of industry as heavy engineering, heavy electrical, heavy chemicals, construction and transport. In other words, reducing the demand for labour to more manageable proportions was accompanied by the beneficial effect of a substantial shift in economic resources to those sections of industry where they could provide the foundations for a rapid advance at a non-inflationary pace which occurred in 1959–60. It must, however, be emphasised that bringing the economy into an equilibrium at which wage costs are not out-pacing productivity is not the same thing as pursuing deflation to the point at which mass unemployment results. There is no reason in theory or in fact why the economy should not expand at a rapid rate without inflation. After all, Germany has demonstrated that this is perfectly feasible. This does not mean that, when surplus capacity exists, it is not the responsibility of the government to give a necessary stimulus to demand. A sound economic policy involves taking steps that are appropriate to time and circumstance.

The lessons of national wages policies

The second reason why inflation cannot be held in check by a national wages policy is simply that in a free society it is impossible to prevent employers from paying higher wages if they wish to do so. I have shown elsewhere that every country which has attempted to control its inflation by means of national wages policy has failed to achieve the success for which it hoped.* The evidence indicates beyond question that it is quite impossible to bottle up an excessive level of demand by sitting on wages. Eventually the pressure blows out and there is a wage explosion which takes the level of wages shooting up. This consequence could only be prevented by totalitarian methods. Thus, in the circumstances envisaged by some writers, a national wages policy could only be successful at the cost of destroying fundamental rights.

For these reasons it is unlikely that a national wages policy which involved the establishment of an all-powerful central authority would be acceptable or workable. It is true that in the Netherlands there exists a centralised control of wages, and that this seems to be compatible with the maintenance of a free society. The reconciliation has, however, in fact been achieved by a constant retreat before the pressure of the unions, and by general economic policies that from time to time have so checked the inflationary expansion of demand as to make the wage controls workable. Certain advantages are enjoyed by the Netherlands: they are the advantages of a corporate state, a high level of social stability and a national tendency to accept the restraint and responsibility made necessary by the fact of being a very small nation and extremely vulnerable to external economic pressures. Since the evidence at home and abroad points to the failure of centralised national wages policies as a remedy for inflation, there would seem to be little reason to adopt a policy of this kind.

The principal need in so far as the aggregate level of wages is

* *National Wages Policy in War and Peace,* Allen & Unwin, 1958.

concerned is that it should not rise faster than the general increase in a nation's output of goods and services. This can only be achieved by an economic policy which must be framed so as to maintain conditions in which it will not be possible for the unions to obtain wages that exceed the appropriate level, since employers will not be in a position to pay them. Does this then mean that the unions bear no responsibility for maintaining a stable and prosperous economy? To come to this conclusion would be to go too far. The unions certainly have responsibilities, but they cannot be expected to carry the responsibility of holding wages down when other incomes are rising. They ought, however, to be prepared to co-operate with other sections of the community in the task of maintaining stability and a high rate of economic growth, and in times of crisis to respond to an appeal for wage restraint.

Since it is extremely difficult to guide a complex economy with such finesse as never to overshoot the mark, inflation and deflation will always be ever-present threats. Moreover, there are factors which are, to a large extent, beyond our control, that from time to time may well give the economy a severe jolt, such as the external cost-push that may be felt through adverse changes in the terms of trade, political pressures and the demands of defence. For example, in such circumstances as those which arose in 1948, when Sir Stafford Cripps asked the unions to exercise wage restraint, the positive response of the unions was certainly helpful. What this period demonstrated was not that wage restraint was unimportant, but that it could only be a temporary relief that could not be sustained without the support of other anti-inflationary measures of a more general economic kind. It would also be much easier in normal times for the unions to pursue a moderate wages policy if it were obvious that employers were obliged to pass on some of the fruits of increased efficiency to the general public in the form of lower prices.

Unfortunately, just as unions have fallen into the bad habit of demanding obviously inflationary wage increases, employers have been encouraged to adopt the equally bad habit of refusing to compete by way of price reductions. Businessmen must, of course, be expected to behave like businessmen, and it would in the normal course of events be just as futile to expect them not to take advantage of favourable market opportunities to secure greater revenue as it would be to expect the unions to forego continuously opportunities to obtain higher wages. Their behaviour in general must be determined by a state of economic affairs in which they are stimulated to act in a manner that is in the public interest, but there are situations in which they ought to put the maintenance of price stability above their short-run profit possibilities. In such exceptional circumstances they ought to be willing to act in a way that is most consistent with the public welfare and their own long-run interests.

It is inevitable in an expanding economy that the service sectors, which cannot increase their productivity at the same rate as the manufacturing sectors, will have to raise prices in order to permit their workers to share in the general prosperity. If over-all stability is to be maintained these price increases must, therefore, be offset by price reductions in the rapidly expanding sections. It follows that workers and shareholders in the manufacturing industries cannot be allowed to take this increment out to the full, since that would leave nothing to be passed on in the form of lower prices. It is, therefore, essential that the elimination of the factors making for monopolistic price policies should be resolutely pursued. This means that the economic, legal and institutional framework must be so adjusted as to make it profitable to all concerned to adopt wage and price policies that do not conflict with the attainment of economic stability. In particular the time is now ripe for the complete abolition of resale price maintenance and the law ought to be changed to achieve this end. There ought also to be a drastic reduction in tariffs, since the high level of protection has done much to create a soft home market in which inefficient and high cost producers can ignore competition and make large profits by raising their prices at will.

Co-operation for information

With these problems in mind there is some attraction in the idea of closer co-operation between the T.U.C., the British Employers' Confederation and the government. If these three organisations could agree through the National Joint Advisory Council on Industry and the Economic Planning Board to issue at regular intervals broad statements on the wage and price situation, this could be helpful to negotiations on both sides.

What I have in mind is nothing as formal as a national collective agreement on the lines of those negotiated in Norway and Sweden between the central federations of employers and unions. It would not be possible under British conditions to enforce such an agreement on individual unions and employers; nor would it be desirable that an agreement of this kind should be supported by compulsory arbitration.* What is required is not greater centralisation of the actual process of wage determination, but a better understanding by unions and employers of the broader economic aspects of their decisions. In particular, it is important that the unions should realise that they cannot secure price stability whilst at the same time demanding that the Government should pursue inflationary economic policies. The essential condition on which price stability and free collective bargaining can be reconciled is an acceptance of the need to use such instruments of economic control as the rate of interest, government spending and taxation, when necessary, in a counter-inflationary fashion. In this respect all that is required of the unions is that they should not insist on inflationary wage increases to the point of plunging the country into a wave of strikes when they meet resistance. This is not to suggest that never under any circumstances should a union strike for higher wages. To give such counsel would be idle and objectionable: idle because it would not be acceptable to free trade unions and objectionable because if accepted it would undermine the basis of free collective bargaining which, in the last resort, rests on the right to refuse to work under an undesired contract.

It will never be easy under a high level of employment in a free society to keep rising costs from becoming out of hand. As a rule of thumb, wages ought not to rise faster in the aggregate than the total output of goods and services, but it will be difficult to avoid overshooting this target. It has been suggested that wage increases should be limited to a figure such as two-and-a-half per cent a year, which is likely to be close to the average rate of economic growth over the long-run period. There is much to commend in this idea, but it has certain grave limitations. A suggestion along these lines was recently made by Lord Chandos, but the pioneer of long-term agreements containing an annual improvement factor, based on an

* A. Flanders, 'Can Britain have a Wage Policy?', *Scottish Journal of Political Economy*, July 1958.

average rise in productivity, was Mr. Walter Reuther, the dynamic leader of the American United Automobile Workers' Union. The first agreement negotiated by Mr. Reuther in which this principle was embodied ran for five years, and it was subsequently renewed for a further three years. In addition to the automatic increase in wages based on the productivity factor, the members of the Automobile Workers' Union were also protected against adverse changes in the price level by a cost-of-living sliding scale. These two things, taken together, guaranteed that employees would have rising real wages of a fixed amount for five years ahead.

It is worthy of note that the U.A.W. agreements were negotiated in a period of expansion, and that the depression in the American motor-car industry has led many industrialists and economists to question the wisdom of these agreements. Opinion on the economic effect of this type of agreement is divided, but it is generally agreed that the effect would be inflationary if productivity failed to rise by the estimated amount and if the additional costs were covered by raising the price of the product. The effect might also be inflationary if this type of agreement were generally introduced without consideration of the very different rates at which production increases in different parts of the economy. Under full employment one of the major problems is to provide for wage increases in the service sector where productivity rises only slowly, without causing price increases that lead to price increases elsewhere. In order to maintain the price level in equilibrium it is necessary for prices to fall in the rapidly growing sections of the economy, since it is only in this way that the benefits of high productivity can be passed on to all sections of the community without causing inflation or inequity. It follows that the unions in the high productivity sector of the economy cannot be allowed to have their wages solely determined by the level of productivity in their own industry. If long-term wage agreements could be coupled with an agreement to pass on any excess profits earned during the period, by at least the same proportion, to the consumer, in the shape of price reductions, they would certainly be an advantageous development.

The problem of an over-rapid rate of increase in money incomes would vanish in some sectors if the general level of employment were not allowed to rise to the point where the demand for labour far outstrips the supply. Given a definition of full employment which recognised that price stability requires an average unemployment over the course of the cycle of two-and-a-half per cent, there is a good chance that relative wage and price changes would settle down at levels that did not provoke inflation.* This would mean that the particular problems of structural unemployment that have long beset areas of England, Scotland and Wales would require specific solutions rather than an increase in the general level of demand to a point that would inevitably produce inflationary results. Whether it is possible to reach this objective only time will tell, but it is one to which enlightened leaders in all parties, whether trade unionists or employers, could rally without sacrifice of their principles and true interests.

If, in order to maintain reasonable price stability, it is necessary to have on the average 500,000 men and women out of work, then there is an obligation on society to do its utmost to ensure that they do not suffer unduly. The magnitude of this problem will, of course, depend on the length of time during which most of them are without jobs. The greatest social hardship arises when workers are unable to obtain employment for long periods. If the majority of those unemployed fall within the short-term category, it should be possible to mitigate their loss to a great extent by an improvement in the level of unemployment compensation. The long-term unemployed who are largely to be found in such areas as South Wales, West of Scotland and Lancashire, are the unfortunate consequence of advancing industrial technology. The answer to structural unemployment in single-industry areas is not to raise the general level of demand to a point at which it will generate an inflationary wage pull in the general labour market but to seek, by specific measures of industrial location, retraining and other forms of direct assistance to deal with the particular problem as it arises.

Differentials

Changes in the aggregate level of wages form only one aspect of the wages problem that has been called in question under conditions of full employment. From the point of view of stimulating maximum productivity, encouraging adequate mobility, greater respon-

---

* Strong supporting evidence for this contention has recently been provided by Professor A. W. Phillips in an article published in *Economica*: 'The Relation between Unemployment and the Rate of Change of Money Wage Rates in the United Kingdom, 1861–1957.'

sibility, and better industrial relations, present wage structures often leave much to be desired.

During the past fifty years wage differentials have altered considerably under the impact of social change, the spread of trade unionism, technological developments in industry and the rise of national collective bargaining. The combined effect of these factors has been to reduce the differentials that traditionally existed between the unskilled and the skilled workers, between the metropolis and other areas, and between manual and clerical occupations.

It is difficult to say precisely how far this narrowing of differentials is due to the activities of the trade unions as distinct from the other factors. The relatively greater increase in the wages of the lower income groups can be explained simply by changes in the supply and demand for different grades of labour, but some writers have suggested that the unions have been mainly responsible. There is reason to believe, however, that the unions have been a secondary rather than a primary cause. Certainly one of the principal objectives of the trade unions has been to establish uniform rates for given occupations, to reduce the difference between industries; and the organisation of the unskilled groups has led to demands for greater equality between the grades. And in both inflationary periods, 1914–20 and 1939–50, when the greatest narrowing took place, the unions asked for and obtained flat-rate wage increases based upon the rise in the cost of living. The effect of raising wages in this way was inevitably to reduce the differentials in percentage terms.

There has been a growing tendency during the past few years to question the wisdom of allowing this trend to continue unchecked. In a number of instances unions have reverted to percentage claims, but in certain cases, for example, printing, railways and London Transport, adjustments of differentials have been accompanied by acute conflicts.

The rigidities of the basic wage rate structure have been greatly eased by the various additions paid by employers so as to bring the actual earnings pattern into closer relationship with market requirements. Although attention is usually fixed on differentials in basic rates it is the actual size of the pay packet that a worker habitually receives that ought to be measured. This is, unfortunately, a difficult task, because the Ministry of Labour refuses to make the necessary surveys of occupational earnings. In this respect the British Ministry of Labour lags far behind the United States Bureau of Labour Statistics.*

This situation in which unions are preoccupied by the level of the basic rate and with flat-rate increases has left the employer relatively free to adjust his wage payments to his local needs. It has been possible to make this job or that job more attractive by the amount of overtime worked, week-end premiums, piece-rate or other bonus earnings. Unfortunately the consequence has been in many cases that wage structure has lost all meaning. Firms have found themselves committed to inefficient and inequitable wages patterns that give rise to constant trouble, and this is only made worse by further twists and shifts of expediency.†

Much of the trouble arises from the character of collective bargaining as it is practised in many industries in Britain today. The principal emphasis is on national agreements, and it is common practice to negotiate a national basic wage rate for unskilled and skilled workers. This crude concept of collective bargaining is far from adequate, and it has, in fact, been recognised as such by the growth of local bargaining and adjustment to meet local needs. This two-tier system of collective bargaining could be much better than it is at present if unions at the local level were better led, better informed and more concerned with establishing sound and equitable wage structures than with merely exploiting local bargaining opportunities. The indictment, as already made clear, also applies to many employers who have been motivated as much as the unions by short-term expedients.

There will, however, have to be considerable changes in the structure and pattern of wages in the future and the problems that are arising are not likely to be solved at the level of national agreements.

The development of modern technology in industry is rapidly reducing the extent to which the individual operative is in sole control of his rate of output. As industry becomes more automated

---

* The inadequacy of British statistics in the field of wages is as notorious as the obscurantism of those, on both sides of industry, who advise the Minister on the information that he should make available to the public. Nothing is more urgently required by students of labour problems than a more enlightened attitude on the part of all concerned.

† See D. J. Robertson, *Factory Wage Structures and National Agreements*, C.U.P., 1960, and *A Market for Labour*, Hobart Paper 12, I.E.A., 1961.

far more capital is employed, and responsibility of the operative for the efficient use of the equipment becomes more significant. With the rise in the capital ratio it becomes necessary to spread the costs of the equipment over the longest possible running time, and it is likely that more shift work will be necessary.

These developments mean that many of the incentive schemes that are currently in use will sooner or later have to be fundamentally revised. If satisfactory wage structures are to be developed, employers and unions will have to study local labour markets and to fix appropriate rates. In addition, relativities will have to be worked out by the most suitable form of job and wage rate analysis, and incentives that are appropriate for the new conditions will have to be found. It will be necessary to develop methods of rewarding adequately and fairly such qualities as responsibility that are difficult to measure. Merit awards which are now made by many firms are often not popular with the unions because they may be used to reward the 'blue-eyed boys'; it is not impossible, however, to devise ways and means of preventing arbitrary and unfair practices. It will also be necessary to pay increased attention to compensation for shift working.

Fringe benefits

By comparison with the situation in the United States, the scope of collective bargaining in Britain tends to be extremely narrow. Whereas British unions are mainly concerned with changes in the basic rates or wages and such aspects of the contract of employment as the basic working day or week, overtime payment and holidays, the American unions have extended their bargaining interests to include a whole range of what they graphically describe as 'fringe benefits'.

Fringe benefits include such items as redundancy agreements, pension and sickness programmes, and profit-sharing schemes.

For several reasons British trade unions have shown relatively little interest in negotiating company pensions, sickness and profit-sharing schemes. In the first place agreements covering these benefits can generally be negotiated only at company level, therefore they are not suitable matters for inclusion in the typical national negotiations. Secondly, pensions and sickness schemes provided by employers have not been in ideological harmony with the welfare-state notions of national insurance and the National Health Service. A third reason is simply that British trade unions are extremely conservative institutions; they rarely innovate and prefer to wait until a need is absolutely manifest.

In the United States collective agreements are legal contracts enforceable in the law courts; in Britain they are merely gentlemen's agreements. The difference is important; it is close to the heart of the contrast in industrial relations in the two countries. Because collective agreements in the United States are legal contracts, American trade unionists and employers work to the letter of the law. Each side compels the other to keep to its contract, and therefore, to 'get it in the contract' is a basic injunction of collective bargaining in the United States. This first principle is no more obvious than in the regulation of dismissals and re-engagements.

Almost every American collective agreement contains detailed provisions relating to the seniority enjoyed by employees. When a firm is compelled to dismiss any of its workers, for reasons other than discipline, it must lay them off strictly according to their length of service, i.e. seniority: modified, of course, by agreed definitions of necessary skill factors to be taken into account. The principle of the last man to be employed to be the first to be dismissed is often used in Britain, but this is generally a matter of custom and practice rather than the result of a carefully worked-out and often highly complex system of seniority rules.

British employers are usually opposed to the seniority principle on the grounds that it is rigid and often leads to unfortunate results. There can be no doubt that there is truth in this contention, but the principle does provide the worker with a clearly (if crudely) equitable rule. It has two other advantages: it encourages the acceptance of labour-saving equipment, since the bulk of the employees in a plant know that they are reasonably secure from displacement by reason of the length of their seniority. It also prevents disputes and strikes over who shall be the ones to go. This important question is decided in advance by the rules, and any dispute over the carrying out of the rules can be arbitrated. In Britain the decision on who shall go is made by the employer and, if challenged by the unions, it may finally be settled by a trial of strength.

It was a natural step from the seniority system to the compensation of workpeople who were disturbed in their employment, by no fault of their own, after they had reached a certain level of seniority. Compensation for unemployment was first conceived as the establishment of a wage packet filled for a whole year, instead of merely an hour, week or month. The guaranteed annual wage is now more commonly referred to in the United States as supplementary unemployment benefit; it lasts under most agreements not for a year but for six months, and under the pioneering agreements in the motor industry a worker laid off was entitled to have his state unemployment benefit increased by the employer to a level which would, for the first few weeks out of work, give him sixty-five per cent and for the next twenty-two weeks sixty per cent of his wages.

British unions have not made very determined attempts to achieve a similar degree of income security for reasons which are easy to explain; they are related to the structure of collective bargaining, to the traditions of reliance on the state for the relief of unemployment, to the opposition of Communist elements among shop stewards who prefer to foster the sterile and stupid slogan of 'no redundancy', and to an habitual conservatism at high levels of union leadership. Those redundancy schemes which exist in British industry have in the main been established on the initiative of employers, and are usually to be found in concerns which have a national reputation as good employers.

There is room for a considerable expansion of this kind of arrangement, and both the Conservative and Liberal parties have stressed the need for longer contracts of service. The present Conservative Government, it is believed, toyed with the idea of giving legislative effect to more comprehensive contracts of service, but in the event it was decided, rightly in my opinion, to seek to encourage rather than compel employers to follow the lead given by those who have set new standards in this respect.*

The advantage of greater employment security is that it encourages loyalty, co-operation and stability in industrial relations. It may tend to lower mobility, but as against that employers are likely to give more careful attention to the planning of their labour needs.

* *Positive Employment Policies*, Ministry of Labour and National Service, 1958.

The net effect could well be a substantial improvement in the efficiency of labour utilisation and a reduction in labour costs.

Pension schemes

Greater security of employment is not the only trend in the conditions of work that is blurring the sharp distinction that previously existed between members of the 'staff' and the hourly paid employees. Superannuation used to be the prerogative of those who were on the staff but about ten million employees are now covered by supplementary pension schemes.

Although there are now proportionately more salaried employees in this total, industrial pension schemes are steadily being extended to cover wage earners. The Labour Party was first to propose that there should be a compulsory and national scheme of superannuation that would, in effect, embrace the voluntary provisions now provided on an industrial basis.*

The Government has accepted the need to extend the provisions for a higher level of retirement income to a wider section of the community than that covered by private schemes, and its own proposals came into effect in April 1961. These are similar in many respects to those originally canvassed by the Labour Party, but they are less bold, and for this reason less likely to incur the danger of requiring the Exchequer to make a contribution that might be inflationary. The Government's scheme is also less certain to discourage a continued expansion of private schemes than the one advocated by the Labour Party.

The remarkable development in supplementary pension schemes, as distinct from the experience in the United States, has not come about in Britain as a result of trade union pressure. The main cause of the rapid growth of industrial pensions in the post-war decade has been full employment and the desire of employers to maintain a stable and loyal labour force. Many trade unionists were inclined to look upon pension schemes as a device to wean union members away from their organisations. All unions have not taken this narrow view, and in the nationalised coal industry the miners quickly demanded a supplementary pension scheme, although it took some time to persuade a majority of miners that it was in their interests to join. As inflation has constantly cut into

* *National Superannuation: Labour's Policy for Security in Old Age*, 1957.

the value of the state pension and the general level of earnings has risen, there has been a gradual change in trade union attitudes. The doctrine of flate-rate contributions and flat-rate benefits was reluctantly abandoned by the Trades Union Congress, after stalwart support for over forty years, in favour of the percentage rates of contribution and benefit embodied in the Labour Party's national superannuation proposals. In the meanwhile, unions are not making supplementary pensions a main feature of their demands, but they are clearly in favour of employers introducing private schemes and in some instances, for example in the building industry, the unions have indicated their desire to see a suitable scheme introduced as soon as possible.

From the point of view of industrial relations there is much to be said for private schemes, since they are clearly identified with the firm, and if the union is associated with the establishment and management of the scheme, as is the case in the United States, it shares in the general satisfaction which accrues. The danger that private schemes might seriously affect labour mobility may well be overcome by Parliament following the suggestion that these schemes should be compelled by law to include the right of transfer when a person moves to a new job.

The establishment of pension schemes necessarily involves questions of financing and investment. So far, in both Britain and America, the unions have not sought to influence the investment of pension funds, and trustees have been guided by orthodox canons of sound investment. The Labour Party has, however, raised the question of using the funds accumulated under its national superannuation scheme for the purpose of acquiring an interest as shareholders in the control of 'blue chip' companies. The unions, who have always been highly conservative investors of their own capital, in spite of having a much wider discretion than other trust funds, have not shown any great enthusiasm for this notion. Mr. Walter Reuther, who has pioneered so many new developments in the field of collective bargaining, has, however, indicated that in future his union might seek a more active share in the management of the gigantic pension funds which are the product of his successful negotiations. The same issues are being actively debated in several European countries and the ultimate outcome may well be a kind of co-operative control over capital development that is quite different from contemporary capitalism or contemporary socialism. Such a development could lead to an extension of the German concept of *Mitbestimmungsrecht,* under which the trade unions are represented on the boards of directors of corporations and have a veto over their labour relations policy. The more unions appreciate the basic features of an efficiently working market economy the better, but there are dangers in them becoming too closely involved in the direction of company investment and price policy.

Profit sharing

Another trend which points in the same long-run direction is the growth of profit-sharing schemes. In a recently published book, Mr. George Copeman has listed and analysed ten different types of schemes in existence in fifty famous firms which enable employees to become shareholders in the enterprise in which they work.* Like many other enthusiasts for employee shareholding and co-partnership, Mr. Copeman over-estimates the effect which the ownership of a small number of shares is likely to have on industrial relations. It is true that, by and large, the level of industrial relations in the firms whose schemes he outlines is better than average, but there is no evidence that this is because employees are actively encouraged and assisted to hold shares. Industrial relations are good because wages are high and the conditions of employment are above average. Employee shareholding is a derivative of the general standard of industrial relations, not the cause of good relations between employees and employers.

The unions have traditionally been hostile to employee shareholding and they have had good grounds for their hostility. After all, when Sir George Livesy, chairman of the South Metropolitan Gas Co., introduced employee shareholding into his concern it was with the avowed purpose of smashing the newly organised Gas Stokers' Union, after the famous victory in 1889, when the union succeeded in having the working day reduced from twelve to eight hours. For many years afterwards the firms which introduced schemes of employee shareholding were mainly of an anti-union, paternalistic type and violated the human dignity of their employees. That unions are no longer actively hostile is due to their

* George Copeman, *The Challenge of Employee Shareholding,* Business Publications, 1958.

own growth in strength and security. They no longer fear profit-sharing schemes, since they have learnt by experience that their members do not regard a share bonus as a substitute for wage increases. So far the majority of employee shareholders would seem to regard the profit-sharing schemes simply as a windfall gain to be turned into cash at once. It is unlikely that any large number of workpeople will, as a result of employee shareholding schemes, become so dependent on this source of remuneration as to consider it as significant to their welfare as their wages and salaries. For this reason employee shareholding is unlikely to become a substitute for the more certain forms of remuneration; it may, however, become an increasingly important supplement.

Over the long run the effect of employee shareholding may well be highly significant, not so much in respect of the relationship of an employee to his supervisor or to higher management, but because of its effects on the system of private enterprise. It is possible that it could undermine the attractions of public ownership, which have rested to a large extent on the false assumption that nationalisation would alter the nature of industrial relations. If privately owned firms not only provide conditions of employment which are as good as or better than those in nationalised industries, and there is no reason why they should not, but also permit employees to share in their profits, it is possible that support for public ownership among workers would dwindle.

Productivity and restrictive practices

More attention paid by the unions to fringe benefits would make the control of inflation a simpler task. Pension, sickness and profit-sharing schemes have great merit, from the point of view of preventing inflation, of deferring benefits until savings have been made to match the outlays. It is unlikely that the unions would agree to take all the potential increment from the annual increase in the net national income in this form, but if only part were acceptable as deferred benefits, considerable sums might be released for investment.

The Trades Union Congress has given much emphasis to the importance of raising productivity as a contribution to the raising of wages, but the significance of undistributed profits as a source of industrial investment is ideologically suspect to 'left-wing' trade unionists. It is extremely important that the crude concept of profit held by many trade unionists should be dispelled. It would be much the best, so long as the major portion of our economy rests on private enterprise, if the T.U.C. emphasised the necessity of healthy profits as the indispensable basis of industrial expansion. This does not mean that unions should stop demanding a fair share; it does suggest, however, that industrial problems would be much easier to resolve in a climate of opinion in which the basic facts were fully understood by both sides.

Productivity is undoubtedly held back by notions based on an outdated analysis of private enterprise. An employee, it is often suggested, works for someone else and not for himself. While this, in one sense, is merely a statement of fact, in another sense it is highly misleading. Every employee works for himself as much as he works for anyone else. Old-fashioned personal incentive schemes recognised this fact in direct fashion, but the complexities of modern industry are rapidly demolishing these simple devices. High productivity is more and more the result of inter-dependence of teamwork and co-operation. In these new conditions the problem of management is much more difficult, since output depends not on the physical efforts of the individual operative, but on good planning, the smooth flow of materials, harmonious human relations, and mutual confidence between every member of the department or production unit.

In the past, unions have sought to protect the interest of their members by methods designed to limit entry into jobs and to restrict output. It is proper that some indignation should be expressed at these practices, but it should be borne in mind that they are highly respectable and practised by the learned professions as well as by business corporations. We should not, in other words, allow indignation to run away with our sense of judgement. The plain fact shown by the overwhelming weight of the evidence before us from all countries is that men cannot tolerate an entirely individualistic system of society. Man is a gregarious social animal who prefers order and certainty to isolation and anarchy. He insists on mitigating the mental and physical strain of constantly facing the vicissitudes of life by the device of collective organisation. Trade unionism arises out of the need felt by men to regulate and control their working environment. Rules and regulations are inevitable; it is when they are imposed in such a way as to do more harm than good that there is need to modify them. Restrictive practices which seek, like King Canute, to hold up the tide of technological progress in the interest of a particular group must be condemned. As a general rule restrictive practices are closely related to the standard of industrial relations and the quality of management. Where industrial relations are good and employees have confidence in their employers, restrictive practices diminish in importance. There are, of course, exceptions; and old memories and traditional practices die hard. Far too often, however, the problem is one of weak and uncertain management, and this is not solved simply by criticising the union. In some well-known cases the unions are conniving at what can be called by no other name than rackets. Unfortunately, so too are managements; so long as both sides find it in their interest to allow the public to suffer this gross exploitation it is difficult to alter this state of affairs. Unions have a right to ask that their members should enjoy a legitimate measure of security of employment at wages which reflect their full worth, but beyond that they have no right to go. When it is clear that union policies are damaging the public interest it is the duty of management to publish the facts and enlist the aid of publicity to get the situation changed.

I do not believe that there is any panacea for restrictive practices. The best antidotes are sound management, sensible unionism, and the development of good industrial relations. Certainly any attempts to break down restrictive practices by such methods as are used in Soviet Russia – that is, by savage rate cutting, by weakening the unions to the point of emasculation, and by denigrating workers as saboteurs for seeking to protect their interests by restriction of output – is to be rejected as utterly indefensible in a free society. In a free society there are bound to be 'restrictive practices' to a certain degree; that is to say, it is a legitimate function of the unions to see that a code of workshop rules and regulations is adopted which will protect the interests of their members. It is indeed a fair criticism of British unions that they have not paid enough attention to codifying properly workshop practice. Many of the out-of-date attitudes and unofficial strikes would disappear if, as is the case universally in American industry, there was a more fully developed and mature system of grievance procedure.

In the long run it is *only* by increasing productivity that real wages can be increased. It is difficult, however, to convince men who are being displaced by technological progress or made redundant by a temporary slackening of demand for labour, that resisting new methods of increasing output cannot advance their standard of life, or indeed protect them from the ultimate effects of failing to produce more efficiently. But there is evidence to show that the unions recognise, to a growing extent, the importance of rising productivity as the major source of increases in wage earners' real income. The actions of the unions are not always consistent with their pronouncements, but the Trades Union Congress has certainly done a great deal to give practical support to this objective. The support given by the T.U.C. to the British Productivity Council, the work of the T.U.C. Production Department, the training courses for union officials and shop stewards, and the constant emphasis given to problems of raising industrial efficiency in the T.U.C. magazine *Labour* are to be highly praised. These positive efforts compare favourably with the much-vaunted production policies of some American trade unions, and they must be weighed in the balance when judging the attitude and actions of British unions.

However, there is an urgent need to innovate more rapidly, and ways must be found to achieve this. The primary responsibility for securing a more rapid improvement in productivity rests upon management, and methods must be found to make for greater efforts. Part of the solution may lie in taxation changes; the prospective alteration in surtax ought to be of help, but there is need to reshape the tax structure still further, perhaps by way of the introduction of the suggested payroll tax and even larger depreciation allowances. It is now widely agreed that far more facilities should be provided for the education of management. In this respect the new Higher National Certificate in Business Studies and the revised Diploma in Management Studies are important steps forward. Much will depend on their vigorous development and the effective co-ordination of the teaching institutions and business.

III

Trade Unions and Industrial Relations

The right to strike

ANY discussion of wages policy inevitably involves consideration of the ethical and economic implications of the collective withdrawal of labour, since the right to strike is the ultimate bargaining weapon in the hands of a trade union. In democratic societies the right to strike is regarded as one of the basic freedoms enjoyed by employees, but the extent to which the exercise of this right is regulated by law varies from country to country.

In keeping with the general British attitude towards industrial relations, there are few legal restrictions on the right to strike in this country. Even public servants are legally free to strike if they wish, but Civil Service unions do not normally have strike funds and they prefer not to exercise this discretion. Even under the 1927 Trade Disputes and Trade Unions Act civil servants were not deprived of the right to strike, although they were forbidden to belong to organisations not mainly composed of employees of the Crown. Persons employed in gas, water and electricity undertakings may be subject to penalties under the 1875 Conspiracy and Protection of Property Act, if they go on strike in breach of contract. Workers in these industries are perfectly free to strike so long as they give the normal period of notice.*

It is quite legal in Britain for a union to call out its members in support of a trade dispute which involves another union. This is not the case, however, in the United States where, under the Taft-Hartley Act, sympathetic strikes are outlawed. But British

* For a more detailed account of the legal aspects of the right to strike, see O. Kahn-Freund, *op. cit.;* and O. Aikin, 'Legal Perspectives', in B. C. Roberts (Ed.), *Industrial Relations: Contemporary Problems and Perspectives.*

trade unions must be careful to ensure that the primary purpose of the strike is a trade dispute within the meaning of the Act; otherwise union officials and members may not be immune from a charge of criminal conspiracy. So long as a strike is about wages or working conditions members and officials are protected by the trade union statutes. A difficulty may arise if, as in the General Strike of 1926, the unions are also concerned to bring about a change in government policy. It it almost certain that a strike primarily directed against the government would be unlawful, and that those taking part in it would be liable to legal action. If, however, pressure is brought to bear on the government only indirectly, then the officials and members are in no danger unless they commit some specific criminal or actionable offence in the course of the strike. Since all large-scale strikes involve a measure of coercion of the government, legal sanction has to be found in their predominant purpose. The predominant purpose may, in fact, change in the course of the strike, as it was alleged was the case in the coal strike of 1926, when the T.U.C. called upon its affiliated unions to strike in support of the miners.*

It was because the legal issues were so complex that the Government tried to define an unlawful strike in more specific terms in the 1927 Trade Disputes and Trade Unions Act. It may be doubted whether in fact the relevant clauses in the 1927 Act successfully clarified the present state of the law. At any rate this was apparently the opinion of Sir Hartley Shawcross, who was Attorney-General when the 1927 Act was repealed in 1946.

The contrast in the number of working days lost through strikes in the decade following the Second World War compared with the number lost in the decade following the First World War has often been pointed out. The difference is at once apparent, as the table overleaf shows, and the improvement may undoubtedly be attributed to better industrial relations.

There are, however, several disturbing aspects about the present situation which pose serious questions for both sides of industry.

In the first place, while the number of working days lost fell greatly after 1926, since the Second World War the number of disputes involving stoppages of work has risen sharply. A large proportion of these strikes have occurred in the coal industry and

* See. O. Kahn-Freund, *op. cit.;* N. A. Citrine, *Trade Union Law.*

Working Days Lost Through Strikes, 1919–60

	No. of stoppages beginning in year	Total No. of workers involved (000)	Aggregate No. of working days lost in all stoppages in progress in year (000)
1919	1,352	2,591	34,970
1920	1,607	1,932	26,570
1921	763	1,801	85,870
1922	576	552	19,850
1923	628	405	10,670
1924	710	613	8,420
1925	603	441	7,950
1926	323	2,734	162,230
1927	308	108	1,170
1928	302	124	1,390
1929	431	533	8,290
1930	422	307	4,400
1931	420	490	6,980
1932	389	379	6,490
1933	357	136	1,070
1934	471	134	960
1935	553	271	1,960
1936	818	316	1,830
1937	1,129	597	3,410
1938	875	274	1,330
1939	940	337	1,360
1940	922	299	940
1941	1,251	361	1,080
1942	1,303	457	1,527
1943	1,785	559	1,808
1944	2,194	826	3,714
1945	2,293	532	2,835
1946	2,205	529	2,158
1947	1,721	623	2,433
1948	1,759	426	1,944
1949	1,426	434	1,807
1950	1,339	303	1,389
1951	1,719	379	1,694
1952	1,714	416	1,792
1953	1,746	1,374	2,184
1954	1,989	450	2,457
1955	2,419	671	3,781
1956	2,648	508	2,083
1957	2,855	1,359	8,415
1958	2,629	524	3,462
1959	2,093	646	5,270
1960	2,797	811	3,008

were in defiance of the union as well as of the Coal Board. Many of the stoppages which happen today reflect weaknesses in the system of industrial relations at the local level. This problem is bound up with the methods of collective bargaining, trade union organisation and the nature of collective agreements, about which more will be said later.

The second disturbing feature of the present situation is the tendency on the part of some trade union leaders to cast doubt on the system of arbitration as an alternative to striking. The danger that arises once a large-scale official strike has begun is that it may extend if it is not quickly settled. Once a strike fever has been worked up, men and women may be brought out on strike by militant hotheads and the situation can easily and rapidly get out of hand. No one looking at past strike waves can fail to be struck by this element of irrationality. It was this reason and also fear of the political overtones that led the General Council of the T.U.C. to give a cool reception to the appeal by Mr. Cousins for help at the time of the London bus strike in 1958.

The economic loss from strikes so far as the community in general is concerned is not very large. It is certainly far less than is caused each year by common colds or public holidays. Nevertheless, large-scale strikes in basic industries, such as transport, coal or electricity, are a much greater threat to the welfare of the nation today than was ever the case in the past. This is because we now have far fewer reserves to fall back upon than we had in the days when we dominated world trade. Strikes of the magnitude of those which occurred in the great industrial upheavals of 1910–14 or 1919–21 would now completely disrupt our economy, shatter the value of the pound, and impose enormous hardships on the general public. Responsible men in all parties and on both sides of industry are well aware of these facts and are much concerned to prevent any such disaster overtaking us.

Compulsory arbitration

The suggestion has been made that compulsory arbitration should be reintroduced so as to safeguard the community against the disruption of its economic life by the trade unions. Little support for this notion is likely to be forthcoming from either side of industry. And there is little to suggest from the experience of Australia, a country which has had experience of compulsory arbitration for half a century, that strikes can be prevented by law in a democratic community. Australia's record of five times the number of working days lost per thousand workers employed, as compared with this country, provides ample proof of this assertion. Indeed, many competent students of industrial relations are of the opinion that compulsory arbitration actually causes strikes in Australia, since it puts a premium on the pitching of extreme claims which then have to be settled outside the industry. Under this system there is no encouragement to bargain realistically, to learn to give and take, and to rub along together.

British employers chafed under the modified system of compulsory bargaining which we had in Britain until the Government decided, in 1958, that it could safely be abolished. It was considered unfair by employers that they could be compelled to honour an award of the Industrial Disputes Tribunal as an implied term of the contract of employment when there was in effect no way of preventing the union from continuing to ask for more as soon as it wished after an award had been made.

An alternative suggestion to compulsory arbitration which has received a considerable degree of support from some Conservatives is the compulsory strike ballot. The proposal here is that a union should be compelled by law to ballot its members and to obtain a two-thirds majority in favour before it could call a strike. This suggestion has the attraction of an appeal to popular democracy, but closer examination reveals several weaknesses. It may well be true that in some strikes a secret ballot would have prevented the stoppage occurring. On the other hand, there is the overwhelming evidence of the National Union of Mineworkers, which insists on a ballot vote being taken before a strike is called; this provision is ignored daily by the members and the union is almost helpless. Not a single strike in the mining industry—and many thousands have taken place—has been called by the union since nationalisation. Moreover, if a union knew that it was compelled to win a ballot vote of its members it would be bound to do everything in its power to exaggerate a dispute in order to persuade its members to vote in favour. Thus the compulsory ballot would be an incentive to exacerbate industrial relations. It might also be a barrier to the settlement of strikes, since it could be argued that it was equally necessary to obtain a similar majority to end a strike and this might be more difficult than the advocates of the idea assume.

There are, in fact, no panaceas which will prevent strikes in a free society. Strikes are the price that we must inevitably pay for the right to bargain collectively. All the evidence suggests that strikes are a complex social phenomenon caused by a variety of factors. This means that the best antidote to industrial conflict is better industrial relations. We have still much to learn about the causes of industrial unrest and until we are more certain why some industries are more strike-prone than others, why strikes occur in waves, and why some unions are more militant than others, it would be wiser to avoid dogmatic opinions about solutions. What we can say for certain is that there is a tremendous responsibility on the part of union leaders to use the strike weapon with the utmost discretion. It was the irresponsible use of strikes that led to their curtailment under the Taft-Hartley Act in the United States, and to the compulsory strike ballot in Australia. If the unions fail to recognise that the price of power is its responsible exercise, there is bound to arise a public clamour for protection against the use of a weapon which can do so much harm to the innocent party.

What ought to be made unequivocally clear by both parties is that no government can stand by and see the economy crippled by a strike in a key industry. In the past both Labour governments and Conservative governments have used troops in the docks and they were right to do so, and it would be their duty to do so again. At the same time it is not their duty always to favour one side or the other, but to try to ensure a fair settlement of the dispute. The art of government in a free society is the ability to reconcile these barely compatible aims.

The role of the Minister of Labour

In this respect the role of the Minister of Labour is of crucial importance. But what should his role be? Over the course of time the tradition has grown up that the proper function of the Minister of Labour is to provide a service to both sides of industry and when necessary to get into the ring with the parties to a dispute

D

so as to help them patch up their quarrel. However, the question arises whether he is merely the servant of the two parties or whether he is also responsible for protecting the public interest. The problem is posed acutely by the government's efforts to keep wages from rising to inflationary levels. In the course of the 1958 bus strike the Minister was severely attacked for not intervening in a fashion that would have brought the strike to an early end, but only at the cost of continuing the rising wage-price spiral.

The position of the Minister under modern conditions is clearly delicate; somehow he must reconcile conflicting interests and points of view. Whilst it is impossible for the Minister to avoid responsibility for the success of the government's general economic policy, whatever it might be, it is also clear that it should not be the function of the Minister of Labour to push this through at all costs. The role of the Minister in respect of industrial disputes is somewhat similar to that of the Attorney-General in relation to the conduct of his legal responsibilities. Whatever the government, whatever the economic situation, the Minister must maintain the confidence of both unions and employers that he will be an impartial umpire.

It might, therefore, be wise to separate the conciliation and arbitration function of the Ministry of Labour from the other duties of the Ministry, setting up, as in the United States, an independent agency to provide this service.

The type of strike that we have been discussing so far is that which takes place as the result of a deliberate act of union policy with a view to securing a change in wages or working conditions. It would be described by an American or continental jurist as a strike over the interests of the parties. There is another type of strike which is not about changes in the terms of employment, but which arises from a dispute about the proper interpretation of the rights of the parties under the terms of employment. In Britain we do not clearly distinguish these two types of dispute, because under British law a collective agreement is not a legally binding contract as it is, for example, in the United States. This means that there is no automatic pressure on the parties to a British collective agreement to settle disputes that might arise by a judicial rather than a bargaining process.

Plant grievance arbitration

There are strong arguments both for and against making collective agreements legally binding documents. Other countries do not suffer from the plethora of unofficial stoppages, which continue to plague some sections of British industry in particular, because the parties are compelled to settle their disputes without resorting to a stoppage of work. In Sweden, since it is illegal to strike during the duration of a collective contract, the parties must, if they have reached a deadlock, submit their dispute to a labour court for decision. In the United States every collective contract makes provision for the private arbitration of disputes arising out of the interpretation of its clauses. There are more than 30,000 arbitrators in the United States who are regularly called upon to settle questions in dispute. Most of these men and women have made a mark in their own professions and have been named by the parties because of their integrity, independence and ability. Private arbitration has now become so much a standard feature of the American industrial relations system that arbitrators now have their own professional bodies, which aim to maintain the necessary level of professional ethics and to provide advice and assistance to companies and unions requiring the services of an arbitrator.

The development of this system has had the important effect of almost abolishing sudden unofficial 'quickies' or 'wildcat' strikes, as the Americans picturesquely describe shop-floor stoppages. Industrial relations are firmly regulated by a system of industrial law that is rigidly interpreted by both sides. Every detail relating to the rights and duties of an operative in the carrying out of his work is written down in the contract. American agreements are, therefore, long and immensely detailed documents which have the same sanctity within the workshop as the constitution has in the nation at large. By this means peace is kept, each side knows exactly where it stands and must abide by the contract. To British observers the system appears hopelessly rigid and far too constricting on management. The answer to this objection by an American would be that the necessity of entering into a binding agreement compels each party to examine its practices, its rights and its obligations in a logical and analytical fashion that leads to the abolition of a good many of the worst kind of irrational obstructions to good industrial relations: obstructions that exist under British conditions only because neither side is prepared to give them up in case it may weaken its bargaining position.

Whether we should go so far in this country as to make collective agreements legally binding on both sides of industry is a matter that is open to much doubt, but there is an extremely strong case for moving in the direction of the American system of workshop arbitration as the final stage of grievance procedure. The first step that ought to be taken is towards codifying company rules and practices in a written document. A similar suggestion has recently been made by the Ministry of Labour in its pamphlet *Positive Employment Policies.* It is suggested in this document that every firm ought to set forth in a handbook the conditions of employment in clear and lucid terms which would enable every worker 'to feel that he is party to a genuine contract of service involving rights and obligations on both sides'. If this step were taken by every firm it would be a considerable step forward to a situation in which frictional strikes were as rare as outbreaks of smallpox.

The conduct of strikes

Friction cannot be eliminated altogether from human relations any more than it can be eliminated from the relationship of two physical objects that are rubbing against each other. Strikes are therefore bound to occur in the best regulated industrial environments. Some people have been seriously alarmed at what they fear may be the development of a rather ugly aspect of industrial stoppages, namely the intimidation of non-strikers by the use of violent measures to prevent them continuing to work.* Before the First World War a number of strikes were characterised by violent scenes and certain incidents culminated in shooting at riotous demonstrators, with fatal consequences. These skirmishes alarmed both sides and in consequence there has been little tendency in modern times on the part of strikers to resort to violence or on the part of the authorities to try to disperse angry men by the display of firearms. When, therefore, some hotheaded strikers exceeded the limits of peaceful picketing and used physical violence in several strikes in 1957 this was naturally widely reported.

There is no reason to believe, in my opinion, that British unions are likely to change their traditional tactics of peaceful conduct in

* cf. *The Director,* September, 1957.

strikes to emulate the behaviour of trade unions in less tolerant and more excitable countries. Nor is there any case for strengthening the law to deal with any incidents that might occur in the heat of dispute. Any act of physical assault or the infliction of malicious damage to property, whether committed in the course of a labour dispute or not, is likely to be a criminal offence or a tort.

'To build a barricade in a street is a criminal offence and also a tort, known as public nuisance, and the same is true of the blocking of the entrance, say, to a factory, either by digging a hole or by erecting an obstruction or by what in America is called "mass picketing".'*

Peaceful picketing is allowed by law as a proper attempt by men on strike to persuade their colleagues to support them. If, however, picketing involves committing a public nuisance, assault or malicious damage, it is a criminal offence. On the other hand, pickets are entitled to try and induce non-strikers to refrain from entering the workshop where there is a strike. They may

'acting on their own behalf or on behalf of a trade union or of an individual employee in contemplation or furtherance of a trade dispute attend at or near a house or place where a person resides or works or carries on business or happens to be, if they so attend merely for the purpose of obtaining or communicating information or of peacefully persuading any person to work or abstain from work'.†

The attitude of the state towards picketing may be summed up as one of neutrality. That is to say, so long as pickets behave with reasonable discretion the law permits them to try to make a strike one hundred per cent effective. Any question of action against pickets who exceed their legal rights lies within the discretion of the police. It would, in my view, be a mistake to attempt to make the law relating to picketing any more onerous than it is now, since this is not necessary to protect public and private interests. It is far better to rely on the good sense of all concerned and to risk an occasional lapse than to try to deter by the threat of draconic penalties that may have a boomerang effect.

* O. Kahn-Freund, 'The Legal Framework,' *The System of Industrial Relations in Great Britain*, ed. A. Flanders and H. A. Clegg, Blackwell, 1954.
† Trades Disputes Act, 1906.

Shop stewards

It is the shop stewards who generally figure most prominently in
local disputes. Since shop stewards are front-line union officers,
this is not surprising; what is astonishing is the extent to which in
certain unions and in certain sections of industry the stewards are
able to act independently of union control. The report of the Court
of Inquiry into the shocking state of industrial relations at Briggs
Motor Bodies Ltd. in 1957 revealed that the stewards had called
over 500 unofficial stoppages in a little over two years. The stewards
had their own independent organisation with an annual net income
of over £7,000. This large sum of money was entirely under the
control of the shop stewards and outside the authority of the head-
quarters of the union.

It may be asked how such a state of affairs can arise. The answer
is to be found in the history of the shop stewards, in the structure
of the Amalgamated Engineering Union and in the system of collective bargaining. Shop stewards emerged in the engineering industry
in the last decades of the nineteenth century when the industry was
going through a rapid technical evolution which threatened the
traditional rights and privileges of the engineering craftsmen. The
union was organised outside the firms in the industry and was
mainly concerned with the establishment of district rates and
general standards of employment. It was not equipped to protect the
interests of the men at the place of work, and as a natural consequence the workers threw up their own spokesman within the workshop to whom they gave the name shop steward.

Since the whole structure of the union was based upon a geographical concept of organisation, the stewards were not easily integrated into the established framework. The development of the
system of shop stewards was not at first actively encouraged by the
national leadership of the unions, since the suspicion had been
aroused that the stewards were intent on pursuing their own policies
rather than those decided upon by the executive and senior officers
of the union. When, during the First World War, the shop stewards
in the engineering industry established an independent organisation
which ignored the official union leaders, the worst suspicions were
confirmed. The shop stewards could not, however, be wished away
and they had to be reconciled with the unions somehow, since

events had proved that they were indispensable if the interests of the men in the workshop were to be protected.

The solution to this awkward problem was found, in the A.E.U., by making the shop stewards responsible to a district committee and the district secretary. This decision had the effect, however, of strengthening the position of the stewards in relation to the branches and of leaving them almost completely free of control in the workshops. Since, in addition, the A.E.U. constitution was designed to prevent strong leadership at the top, the task of national leaders was not made easy.

If collective agreements were made legally binding, strikes called by shop stewards would render the union liable to be sued for any damages that the employer might suffer from a breach of contract. Since there are few unofficial strikes in countries where collective agreements are binding in law, it is likely that change in this direction would rid British industrial relations of one of its most ugly features. It is certainly anomalous that unions can inflict serious damage on employers and the community in breach of contract without being liable for the harm that they do. Whilst it would be entirely wrong to seek to prevent strikes by making collective stoppages criminal offences or limiting the right of employees to refuse to work under an unfavourable contract, there can be no moral objection to either unions or employers being compelled to honour their agreements or pay damages to the other when they fail to do so.

A number of unions have come to realise the important position which their stewards occupy in modern industry, and in recent years they have given some attention to the problems of communication and training. The Transport and General Workers' Union, in particular, has made a tremendous effort to give all its stewards the opportunity of attending its training courses. Other unions have not made as big an effort and some have done nothing at all. Training and education is unfortunately still too often looked upon as a luxury, as something that is fashionable but not really essential. It is difficult to measure success and it is sometimes painfully obvious that results cannot be guaranteed. Frequently union leaders do not realise that training and education programmes serve as important channels of communication with the key rank-and-file members. When the training is done by the full-time union officials, they help to establish a close relationship between the official and the steward that is far more difficult to establish by routine contacts.

The behaviour of shop stewards is not, however, merely due to inadequacies of union structure, to poor communications, lack of training and weak national and district leadership; it is also a function of the character of the industry and employers concerned. It has been said that employers get the shop stewards they deserve; this compliment might equally be reversed. Tough employers breed tough stewards and vice-versa. Once the kind of tradition that is still distressingly frequent in the engineering and certain other industries becomes established, it is extremely difficult to alter. Mutual suspicion dies hard, and before it passes away its baleful influence retards the development of better relations.

Joint consultation

In the Second World War vigorous attempts were made to bring about an improvement in the relations between shop stewards and management through the medium of joint production committees. Similar attemps had been made in the First World War and the Committee on the Relations between Employers and Employed, better known as the Whitley Committee, recommended in a series of notable reports that, among other steps that should be taken to improve industrial relations, employers and unions should establish joint industrial councils and joint works committees.

Many committees were established, but the majority failed to survive in the economic climate of the 1920's and 1930's. A similar demise of wartime production committees occurred in 1945, but under the conditions of prolonged full employment many committees were revived to carry on the practice of joint consultation. A further impetus to the idea of joint consultation was given when in each of the nationalisation acts it was laid down as a statutory requirement that appropriate machinery should be established for this purpose.

Perhaps far too much was expected of joint consultation, but it has not proved to be the panacea which its protagonists hoped to see. Joint consultative committees serve a useful purpose, but in neither public nor private enterprise have they proved a substitute for effective management.

One of the most important reasons why joint consultative committees have not proved as useful in improving the climate of industrial relations as was expected is that they are not easily related to the negotiating machinery. The unions have spoken loudly in favour of joint consultation, but their protestations of support have concealed important reservations. In the first place the question arises whether every employee, irrespective of union membership, should be entitled to elect members of the committee; secondly, whether committtee membership should be confined to union members; thirdly, what relation the shop stewards should have to the committee; fourthly, whether the committee should be entitled to discuss questions that may also be the subject of collective bargaining and where the line between consultation and negotiation should be drawn; fifthly, what powers the committees should enjoy. All these issues bear upon the functions and powers of the unions at every level of their activity, and unions are naturally not prepared to see them answered in a manner which in any way threatens to weaken their position. Consultative committees have, therefore, in practice generally turned out to be an extension of collective bargaining. As a result it is almost a universal experience to find management complaining that the union members do not understand the purpose of consultation. Union members, in fact, understand the purpose of joint consultation extremely well; they see it as a means of securing improvements in their working conditions and they do not worry too much about the proprieties and formalities of union-management relations. Employers, for their part, are inclined to look upon joint consultation simply as a channel of communication and a managerial tool. Given the pattern of institutional arrangements in industry, the traditional concepts and values of both management and labour, it is not surprising that joint consultative committees have not easily been assimilated into the general corpus of industrial relations.

Many authorities are now coming to the point of view that the proliferation of committees does little to improve industrial relations. The really important factors are simply the quality of leadership on both sides and the confidence each has in the other. These intangible but fundamental aspects of industrial relations are revealed in countless ways in the day-to-day process of decision making, in the attitudes of management and men, in the recognition of the mutual responsibilities, rights and duties of each in the total pattern of industrial relations. The secret of success in industrial relations is in fact to be found in the exercise of those same virtues which have made Britain one of the most stable political communities in the world: tolerance, patience, respect for the rule of law, and a preference for the pragmatic rather than the theoretical solution to problems of human discord. Above all, management must be efficient, fair and firm. No matter what the attitude of the unions might be it is, in the last resort, the standard of management that determines the standard of industrial relations.

IV

Trade Unions and Politics

So far we have been discussing the efforts of the trade unions to obtain higher wages and better working conditions by means of their industrial activities. The unions do not, however, confine their activities to collective bargaining with employers; they seek to influence the policy of governments and to secure legislation in the interests of their members. As political pressure groups, the unions exert their influence in the main through two organisations, the Trades Union Congress and the Labour Party. The T.U.C. is much the older of the two bodies, and, from a strictly trade union point of view, the more important of the two; we shall, therefore, consider it first.

The role of the T.U.C.

There are 183 trade unions affiliated to the T.U.C. and each is entitled to send one delegate for every 5,000 members to the annual meeting of the Congress. This gathering is constitutionally the supreme policy-making authority of the trade union movement, but the key decisions are usually made by the thirty-five-man General Council, which meets at monthly intervals throughout the year. The Council is representative of the Congress as a whole, but each member is nominated from one of the eighteen trade groups into which the unions are divided for this purpose. The object of this method of election is to ensure that every section of the trade union movement is represented, but, at the same time, to prevent any union enjoying a pocket borough. No system of voting can entirely prevent gentlemen's agreements which make the result of an election a foregone conclusion, and there is something of the atmosphere of a well-run club in the election of the General Council which makes prediction of the result generally a relatively easy matter. Those who have been trying for years to obtain a seat on the Council and have not succeeded tend to be critical of the present methods of election, but the majority seem reasonably satisfied that the system now in use, which was evolved after much trial and error, is about as fair and reasonable as can be devised.

The work of the General Council, according to the constitution, is primarily to promote and co-ordinate industrial action, to watch and institute legislation, to adjust disputes between affiliated unions, to carry on propaganda and education, and to enter into relations with trade union and labour movements in other countries. The functions and the powers of the General Council are widely and, except in certain respects, vaguely drawn. The Council has plenty of room for initiative and discretion; it is fettered in practice only by the willingness of its members and Congress to sustain any policy it may choose to adopt.

Perhaps the greatest test which the General Council has had to face was the General Strike of 1926; it managed to survive this challenging, but uninspiring, affair without losing as much prestige as might have been expected. It was during the Second World War that the General Council of the Trades Union Congress really achieved its present eminence as a most influential national body. During the war, with Mr. Bevin at the Ministry of Labour and with Sir Walter (now Lord) Citrine as General Secretary, the T.U.C. was brought into the highest councils directing the nation's efforts to defeat the Nazis. The arrangements which were made to allow the trade unions to participate in the conduct of the war effort were carried on into the peace by the Labour Government. Today the T.U.C. is represented on a very large number of public and private committees dealing with all manner of industrial, economic, social and educational problems.

Perhaps the most important of these bodies are the National Joint Advisory Council on Industry, the National Advisory Council to the Ministry of Labour, the British Productivity Council, and the International Labour Organisation. Through these and kindred bodies the T.U.C. General Council is able to exert a continuous influence and to mould opinion at an important stage in the process of policy making.

In matters of critical importance and public urgency, the General

Council is able to obtain access to the Prime Minister and his Cabinet colleagues without difficulty. It is important to note that the T.U.C. is now recognised by Conservative as well as Labour governments as the union of the unions and the spokesman of the whole body of organised labour.

The consultative role played by the General Council of the T.U.C. in national affairs is not to the liking of the old-fashioned type of trade unionist who longs for the simpler and cruder type of class warfare. With power goes responsibility, and there is no escape from this consequence of the position which the T.U.C. now occupies. The issue before the T.U.C. was starkly posed when Mr. Cousins, at the time of the London bus strike, asked the General Council to support his organisation by calling upon other unions to come out on strike. The Council then faced a crucial choice: it could either go back on all the tremendous gains that it had made in prestige and influence in the past thirty-two years since the fateful days of the General Strike, or resolutely cast that philosophy finally aside. It chose the latter course and, with due respect to Mr. Cousins's sincerity, in the light of past experience it would be widely agreed that it chose rightly.

Some trade unionists see the relations between the T.U.C. and the government entirely in party political terms. Thus in their opinion, a Conservative government is by definition antipathetic to the goals of the unions and should, therefore, be fought by every weapon available, including the strike. This view conflicts with the fundamental position adopted by the T.U.C. ever since the General Strike; its view is essentially that the unions cannot challenge the right of the government to govern as it thinks proper to the circumstances. This does not, of course, mean that the T.U.C. should not voice its opinions vigorously. Nor does it mean that the unions should not seek to exercise political pressure through their support of the Labour Party.

The position of the T.U.C. was well put in 1951, immediately following the election of the Conservative Government, in a statement issued by the General Council:

'We shall continue to examine every question solely in the light of its industrial and economic implication. The Trade Union Movement must always be free to formulate and advocate its own policies. In the future as in the past we shall urge on the Govern-

ment those policies which, from our experience, we believe to be
in the best interests of the country as a whole and from the same
standpoint we shall retain our right to disagree and publicly
oppose the Government where we think it is necessary to do so.'

A similar position had been taken by the General Council in
1938 when it passed a resolution which placed on record its conviction that

'in dealing with any Government on behalf of the Trade Union
Movement its conduct must be determined by industrial and not
political considerations'.

The position of the T.U.C. is inevitably an awkward one when the
bulk of its affiliated membership belongs to unions which are also
affiliated to the Labour Party. Since the T.U.C. must protect the
interests of its member organisations under every government, whatever its party colour might be, the General Council cannot play the
role of official opposition whenever the Conservatives are returned
to power. However, it is impossible to overlook the fact that the
ideological sympathies of the unions lie closer to the Labour Party
than to the Conservatives. The T.U.C. is, therefore, likely to be
more critical of the performance of a Conservative government
than it is of a Labour government. It would be a mistake, however,
to assume that the T.U.C. is in any way a creature of the Labour
Party or vice versa.

Relations with the Labour Party

The T.U.C. is only indirectly linked to the Labour Party through
the National Council of Labour. This body, which has no executive
authority, is mainly looked upon as a useful forum for the private
discussion of matters of common interest. Relations between the
General Council of the T.U.C. and its staff and the Labour Party
tend to be much closer when the Party is in opposition than when it
is in government. During each of the three past Labour governments relations with the T.U.C. became somewhat strained. It is inevitable that this should happen, since the government must act in
the interest of all sections of the community, not merely of the
unions. There are also most subtle reasons why conflicts occur;
trade unionists do not like the implied assumption made by Labour

Ministers that they know as well or better than the unions what is good for wage earners.

From 1945 to 1951 the control of inflation and especially wages policy proved an intractable problem. For a time the unions reluctantly agreed to co-operate with Sir Stafford Cripps in a heroic effort to check inflation. The success of this policy was limited and in spite of urgent appeals from Sir Stafford's successor, Mr. Gaitskell, the unions abandoned their commitment. It is now recognised more clearly than ever that a future Labour government will be faced by an extremely difficult problem if it is to hold prices stable. Somehow it will have to win and hold the co-operation of the unions. The magnitude of the task has already been realised by Mr. Harold Wilson and by Sir Alan Birch, the late chairman of the T.U.C. Economic Committee. Both of these key figures have indicated that they would be in favour of some kind of national wages policy. The merits of such schemes have been discussed earlier; what we are concerned with here is the political possibility of such an arrangement and its repercussions on relations between the unions, the government and the Labour Party.

It can be stated with certainty that any attempts to control wages by decree, by a national wages board or some other form of administrative arrangement, is doomed to failure and would, if it were tried, create an immense rift between the trade unions and the government.

It is claimed by the Labour Party that if it were in office it would create an economic climate in which it would be possible to obtain much greater support from the unions for policies that would achieve stability. The essence of this claim is that the Labour Party would stimulate a much more rapid growth in production which would permit a rate of wage increase that would keep the unions satisfied without being inflationary. It is difficult to see how this objective could be realised by refusing to cut back the level of demand when it surges too high to maintain stable prices. There is no difficulty in stimulating the economy, as we were made well aware after the hire purchase restrictions were taken off in 1958. The problem is to stimulate output without stimulating an excessive rise in wages and profits and also to ensure that the expansion brings about a larger rise in exports than imports. If a Labour government were in office and demand got out of hand, as it almost certainly would, it would have to take positive steps to check the inflation and repair the damage done to the balance of payments. At this point the pursuit by a Labour government even of policies which fell far short of such radical innovations as the establishment of a centralised system of wage determination, to check an inflationary level of demand, would give rise to acute conflict within the Labour movement. If the methods chosen were similar to the methods used by the Conservatives, such as 'tight' money, budget surpluses, restrictions on capital expenditure, and so forth (and it is difficult to see what alternatives the government could use), they would arouse the same kind of antagonism as experienced during the recent past when the glitter was rubbed off the home-consumption boom. The trade unions have every right to criticise the government when they think that its policy is inimical to the interests of their members and the general public, but they have a duty to state exactly how they would cope with the problem. So far they have given the impression that they are more concerned with scoring ideological points off the Conservatives than with the objective facts of the situation.

The difficulty in which the unions are likely to find themselves arises out of a fundamental ambiguity in their political position. When the unions established the Labour Party they did so to achieve a legal framework within which they could carry out their traditional functions, use their normal methods of collective bargaining and, when necessary, strike action. With the adoption of socialism as their aim, however, they embraced an ideological goal which could only be achieved at the expense of the functions which they formed a Labour Party to protect.

The failure of the unions and of the intellectual wing of the Labour Party to recognise the dilemma which confronts the unions leads inevitably to muddled thinking, internecine conflict and charges of dishonesty, hypocrisy and betrayal of the Party's ideals. The position in which the unions find themselves is extremely uncomfortable, and sooner or later events will compel them to resolve it. The choice which lies before the unions is either to come to terms with *laissez-faire* collectivism and to accept the existence of private enterprise and a market economy as a desirable system, since it is only under these conditions that free trade unionism can flourish, or to accept the implications of the ideology of socialism, which would involve the abandonment of free bargaining, the right to strike and the exercise of political pressure – in short to become an agency of the state.

It is not possible to say with certainty which way the unions will go, but in the absence of a cataclysmic upheaval such as a third world war there is reason to believe that in practice they are likely to obstruct rather than to assist those members of the Labour Party who wish to achieve its ultimate doctrinal aims.

Paradoxically it is the trade union leaders who so vehemently assert their allegiance to socialist principles who are most likely to refuse to accept the limitations on their freedom which the attainment of their philosophy would entail. For example, it was the extreme left-wing unions, the Electrical Trades Union, the Foundry Workers' Union and the Boilermakers' Union which opposed the continuance of wage restraint under the last Labour Government, and it is Mr. Cousins who has made it clear that he cannot commit his union to a national wages policy under the next Labour Government, unless he has guarantees that it will not be able to give. It is also not without significance that the union which was the most ardent advocate of an extreme socialism thirty years ago, namely the National Union of Mineworkers, now emphatically asserts its independence of the National Coal Board, and permits its members to behave with a degree of freedom that makes socialist planning almost impossible.

The irony of the present situation in which the Labour Party is seriously divided, perhaps mortally divided, between those who support its leader and those who hold extreme socialist opinions is that the division has been largely brought about by the same union leaders. Whichever way things go it is difficult to believe that the policy which the left-wing unions stand for can be realised.

If the Labour Party is defeated again by the Conservatives it may be destroyed as an effective political force. The pressure of the left-wing unions could make impossible the adoption of a policy the electorate would support; the majority of union members would then lose interest in their affiliation to the Party.

If, on the other hand, a party leadership that commands public support survives and a new unity is forged, there might within a few years be another Labour government. It is unlikely that such a government would attempt to make giant strides towards a fully

E

planned socialist economy, but there might well be serious conflict between the unions and the party leaders, as there was under previous Labour governments over economic policy. It would be surprising if the clash of opinion led to a complete rupture in the relations between the unions and the Labour Party, but another period of Labour government could demonstrate what many people feel has already been demonstrated, that there is really not much difference to be made to the unions whichever party is in power. What could easily emerge is a system of politics in which both parties accepted by pragmatic experience the same conventions, including the position of private enterprise and scope of state planning. Another alternative, which is possible in the long run, is that the Liberal Party might gain back from Labour the support it lost in the first few decades of the century. If this development were to occur the unions might well feel that they had little to gain from a party in political decline and decide to revert to the more independent position they occupied in the nineteenth century. Before the foundation of the Labour Party the unions were politically extremely active and closely associated with the Liberal Party, but they had no direct control or even much influence over the Liberal caucus and constituencies. The long-term trend in the relations of the unions to the political parties in Britain could then lead to a situation not very dissimilar from that which exists in the United States. In America, the unions are not committed by organic ties to one political party; they support candidates from both parties, but they incline closely to the Democrats, who can usually count on winning the bulk of the organised labour vote.

The political levy

There are some people who feel that the unions should not be allowed to play any role in politics and in particular that they should not be able to collect political contributions without obtaining the signature of every member wishing to contribute.

Those who desire to curb the political power of unions are, in practice, usually against the unions because of their attachment to the Labour Party. Once it has been granted that the unions should be free to spend money on political activities it would be difficult to censure them for supporting the party of which they approve.

The activities of the unions in the political field are fairly closely supervised by the Registrar of Friendly Societies, with whom all political rules must be deposited and approved before they become effective. It might indeed be asked why the unions should be controlled in this way. Why should they not be free to spend their money as they choose without having to go through the process of establishing a separate fund, adopting special rules, and being subject to the jurisdiction of the Registrar? The answer is obvious: the unions exercise great power and influence and the community must be protected from the indiscriminate use of funds subscribed to secure industrial protection for political purposes. By their protection of the right to 'contract out' of payment of the political levy, the political rules emphasise the subsidiary character of political activity. Although unions are bound to be involved in politics, since the government of the day can affect their rights and objectives profoundly, politics is a secondary and not a primary activity of trade unions that have achieved a settled position and a high status in the life of a nation. The first duty of a union is to protect the vocational interest of its members by negotiation and consultation; it is only when these methods prove inadequate that the union should enter into politics.

The objection is sometimes raised that it is unfair for the unions to affiliate to the Labour Party when a large proportion of their members vote for other parties. This exercise of the majority rule may be repugnant to the spirit of democracy, but it is not contrary to the law or to accepted practice. Union members may, after all, contract out of paying, and they are free to propose alternative policies. There is, however, a stern duty on the unions to ensure that the member in the minority should not be victimised in any way by bigoted zealots. In this respect the law lays down firmly the principle that no union member must suffer any disadvantage other than not having any say in the government of the political fund, should he contract out of payment.

It is, of course, possible that in certain cases non-levy-paying members may be subject to pressure and discrimination. There is no evidence, however, that this is a serious problem that calls for any revision of the law as it now stands. In order to protect the individual member, the 1913 Trade Union Act lays down that each union must adopt rules for the political fund that conform to the model approved by the Registrar.

'If any member alleges that he is aggrieved by a breach of any rule relating to the political fund he may complain to the Registrar of Friendly Societies. The Registrar, after giving the complainant and any representative of the union an opportunity to state their case, may make whatever order he thinks just under the circumstances to remedy the breach. Such an order is legally binding and conclusive on all parties without appeal and may not be removed or restrained by any Court of law.'

The politics of trade union democracy

We have been concerned so far with the exercise of political pressure by trade unions in an endeavour to achieve goals determined by their principal objectives which arise out of the vocational interest of their members. The external politics of trade union activity naturally mirror the internal politics of trade union government and it is necessary to consider both aspects to obtain a complete picture of the situation.

Although trade unions seek to influence political activities by pressure on governments and the political parties, they do not govern themselves through a party system. The basic principle of trade union democracy in Britain is simply the majority rule of 'unorganised' individual members. Any attempt to form an organised political party for the purpose of contesting union elections is generally frowned upon, and most unions have rules which specifically forbid the kind of political party activities that are regarded as normal in national or local authority elections.

This attitude derives from the basic principle of organisation on which British trade unions rest, namely, that of protecting the industrial interest of members as employees, irrespective of race, creed, colour or politics. It is, therefore, as an employee that a person is entitled to join a union, and any other factor is purely incidental to this essential and central fact of union membership. Since the primary objective of trade union activity is the protection of their members' vocational interest, the attainment of political goals is a subsidiary aim. From this it follows that unions endeavour to choose their governing bodies from men and women who stand on their record as trade unionists and not as supporters of a a particular political party or theory.

This concept of trade union democracy is based on a simple theory of trade union purpose and organisation which served well in the early days of trade union development. It is now open to several objections which derive from the fact that (1) the aims and functions of trade unions have now become extremely complex and (2) the scope of union organisation has vastly expanded and the system of government and administration is entirely different from what it was when the unions were in the Greek city-state stage of development. What is perhaps of even greater importance is the undeniable evidence that union elections in practice are often conducted on political lines.* In many unions there has grown up a *sub rosa* system of party political organisation.

There is nothing new in the attempt of supporters of a particular party to capture the leadership of the unions. In the latter part of the nineteenth century there was a running battle between Liberals and Socialists which finally culminated in the victory of the latter. Today, it is mainly members of the Communist Party who seek to win control of the unions, but Conservatives, Liberals and Roman Catholics are also actively engaged in pursuing their political ends through organised group participation in union elections. It is the Communists, however, who are most active and who, because of their clandestine methods and rigid discipline, are able to take most advantage of the prevailing fiction that union elections are conducted on a non-political basis.

Many exposures of the methods used by the Communists to gain power in the unions have been made in recent years in the Press and on television.† It is also well known that non-Communist groups have taken to organising their members in secret so as to defeat the Communists at their own game. Although counter-organisation has successfully defeated Communist attempts to obtain power, and even removed entrenched Communist officials from office, there is a reluctance on the part of many trade union members to take part in this kind of secret political game. It would be far more healthy if unions could be persuaded to bring internal political conflict right out into the open and to permit electoral activities on political lines.

The strongest opponents of open-air politics in the unions are

* For a detailed discussion of the politics of union elections see my *Trade Union Government and Administration in Great Britain*, G. Bell & Sons, 1956.

† Above all in the evidence and judgement given in the case involving the fraudulent election of the General Secretary of the E.T.U.

naturally those who gain most from the present hole-in-the-corner system. It is perhaps not surprising that those unions which are strongly influenced by the Communists, such as the Electrical Trades Union and the Amalgamated Union of Foundry Workers, have been the most insistent on the maintenance of their rules which forbid canvassing, 'outside interference' and unauthorised communication within the union. The rules which were devised to prevent the organisation of minority groups and the exclusion of political influence can be used to safeguard the position of a ruling clique from the efforts of a dissident group to dislodge it.

The Communists are always quick to appeal to the democratic sentiments of the majority of trade union members whenever it is suggested that the political affiliations of candidates should be stated openly on union ballot papers. The whole problem was clearly brought out at the 1958 annual conference of the Union of Post Office Workers. At this conference a resolution was moved to compel candidates for the union's Executive Council to declare their political affiliations. The proposer stated that most members of small union branches never knew what kind of person politically they were voting for, and that they were entitled to this knowledge if they were to judge properly the qualifications of a candidate for office. The debate which followed exhibited the confusion into which liberal democrats often fall when faced by the unpalatable facts of Communist political behaviour. It was suggested that to compel candidates to declare their political affiliation violated the fundamental canons of free speech and freedom of political activity. Faced by divisions within their own ranks the Executive Council could not arrive at a unanimous conclusion and therefore made no recommendation. In the event, the amendment was carried by a show of hands, but lost on a card vote with a substantial minority not voting.

The extraordinary aspect of this debate was the stubborn refusal of well-meaning people to accept the plain fact that the Communist Party is a conspiracy designed to destroy democracy for ever. It is difficult to understand why it should be thought democratic to perpetuate a system which permits members to be deceived. It is also difficult to understand why it should be regarded as 'witch hunting' to make a candidate for office declare his interest. Opposition to a declaration of political allegiance on these grounds is tantamount to admitting the truth that Communists are not likely to obtain office if their politics are known. Why it should, therefore, be thought to be in the interests of democracy that the wishes of the majority should be deliberately thwarted by keeping them ignorant is a question that can only be answered in terms of a perverse notion that the majority in this case is merely the victim of prejudice and false assumption. It is one of the most extraordinary facts of our time that many democrats with the best of intentions are willing to violate fundamental principles of democracy to prevent Communists from being defeated by force of public opinion.

The way in which Communists are sometimes prepared to obtain office was spotlighted some years ago in a study of a Communist-dominated branch of the Transport and General Workers' Union.* Events in other unions more recently have shown that Communists are quite prepared to violate democratic practices when defeat stares them in the face. The unease aroused by revelations of malpractice has led to suggestions that Britain should follow the example of Australia and adopt legislation which would enable official inquiries to be made into allegations of electoral fraud.

The prevention of electoral malpractice

This Australian legislation was first passed in 1949 by a Labour government, with the support of the Australian Council of Trade Unions, following the report of a Royal Commission which revealed that Communists had ruthlessly violated union rules to maintain power. The Act provided (1) that any member of a union could file an application with the Registrar of Trade Unions for an inquiry into alleged irregularities; (2) that the Registrar must decide whether there were reasonable grounds for an inquiry; (3) that the judge appointed by the Court to undertake the inquiry should have powers of subpoena; (4) that the judge might at the conclusion of his inquiry (a) declare the election void, (b) declare that someone else had been elected, (c) order a new election under such safeguards as he deemed necessary; (5) that a union might ask the Registrar to conduct its elections if it had reason to believe that irregularities would otherwise occur.

It was soon obvious that there were certain defects in this legis-

* J. Goldstein, *The Government of British Trade Unions*, 1952.

lation, and when the Conservatives were returned to office they amended the Act in 1951. Under the original Act the power to ask the Court to conduct an election without a judicial inquiry rested with the union, but it had become obvious that a union already dominated by Communists was unlikely to ask the Court to interfere. The Act was therefore amended so as to permit the Arbitration Court to conduct union elections on the application of any group of members, so long as they numbered not less than 1,000 or one-tenth of the total membership. Other amendments to the Act required that all unions should make constitutional provision for secret ballots, and gave the Court power to conduct a secret ballot of union members whenever it considered that by so doing it might prevent or lead to a settlement of an industrial dispute.

These amending measures went farther than the Labour Party or the trade unions could stomach, and they were strongly opposed, but without avail. This legislation appears to have led to the defeat of Communist leaders previously well entrenched. It has not, however, entirely eliminated the Communists from office, and they still exercise a considerable degree of influence in Australian unions. It appears to have had no significant effect on the militancy of the unions. The number of strikes has tended to decline, but this may be due to other factors.

The problem of the unrepresentative government of unions has given rise to much concern in the United States in recent years. There the question does not centre on the danger of Communist control, although this was a very real issue some years ago when some of the most important unions were dominated by Communist cliques. Nowadays the problem is that of preventing unscrupulous opportunists from obtaining power, and then, in association with underworld elements, exploiting union members, employers, and the public in the amassing of huge personal fortunes. Under changes in the law introduced by the Labour Management Reporting and Disclosure Act far-reaching regulations of the government and administration of unions have been brought into effect.*

The most important aspect of the Australian legislation is undoubtedly the power to conduct a judicial inquiry into situations in which there is evidence of a flagrant abuse of union rules by unrepresentative factions; this is also an important feature of the

* See Part II, Chapter IV.

recent amendments to the law in America. The Minister of Labour in this country has no power to order such an inquiry, nor does the Registrar have any power to intervene when it is alleged the union's rules are violated. Members could, however, seek from the Courts a declaration that an election was null and void, and an injunction to restrain the union from acting in breach of its rules. In circumstances in which internal union politics were leading to industrial unrest the Minister could set up a Court of Inquiry to investigate, as he did in the notorious case of Briggs Motor Bodies.* Although it would be wrong to exaggerate either the extent to which Communists dominate British unions, or the extent to which elections are fraudulently manipulated, there is a fairly strong case for amending the law in Britain so as to permit aggrieved members of any union, whether registered or unregistered, to complain to the Registrar of violations of union rules in any context, instead of, as at present, only in the case of the rules which apply to the political fund. To make the powers of the Registrar effective it would be necessary to limit the legal privileges of trade unions to registered organisations; and further it should be made clear in the law that unions would not be registered unless their rules conformed to standards that satisfied the requirements of 'natural justice' and the preservation of the rights of union members. It should also be possible for the Minister to appoint a fact-finding Court of Inquiry, on the recommendation of the Registrar, which would issue a public report on the conduct of the union and, if necessary, make suggestions as to the reform of the rules of the union concerned.

In view, however, of the general absence of corruption in British unions and the usually high standard of conduct of internal union affairs, the most satisfactory course would be for the unions themselves to make entirely certain that their members have no grounds for legitimate complaint. This is not a difficult task; unions could easily safeguard their reputation and their members' interests by establishing an independent appeals procedure. Although there is no reason to believe that in the majority of cases union executives do not exercise their authority with fairness and wisdom, it is contrary to the principles of justice that a governing body should be a judge and jury of a case in which it may have a powerful interest. There are two feasible possibilities; there ought to be

* Cmd. 131, 1957.

established either a central appeals committee under the auspices of the T.U.C., or unions might follow the lead of Mr. Walter Reuther, who has set up a committee of seven prominent citizens, who have no connexion with the union, to whom any member might appeal if, after exhausting the union's machinery, he is not satisfied that he has had a fair deal. British unions are not likely to receive a suggestion of this kind with enthusiasm, since they have a morbid fear of outside interference. They must, however, realise that they now occupy a far too powerful position in public life to remain immune from public interest in their internal affairs or from the public's right to insist that they should take such steps as will ensure that their power is not, even inadvertently, abused.

It is impossible to discuss the problem of union democracy and the protection of the rights of union members without reference to the E.T.U. case. After lengthy hearings Mr. Justice Winn came to the conclusion that the union's election process had been violated by certain leaders of the union who were members of the Communist Party. An appeal against the findings of the Court was abandoned, but whatever the ultimate outcome of this case it was admitted by the defendants that the union's rules had been violated and the election of the General Secretary was null and void.

The E.T.U. case once again underlines the vital role of the Courts in the regulation of trade union activities, but the magnitude of the case also illustrates the need for the kind of reforms discussed earlier. The reaction of the General Council of the Trades Union Congress to the findings of the Court proved to be firmer than was expected; but this decision also illustrates the need for the T.U.C. to have increased authority over affiliated organisations. The tradition of almost absolute autonomy must give way to the need for the trade unions to measure up to the problems of the present.

Apathy

It is often suggested that the problem of political democracy within the unions would be solved if a majority of members bothered to vote in union elections, to attend union meetings and to voice criticism. Clearly, the fact that only a very small proportion of members does take an interest in the government of any union is a very serious menace to the survival of democracy, but more is required than a large vote or large turnout at a meeting. The members must be made aware of the issues involved and sufficiently stimulated to consider that to take an active interest in union affairs is worth while. No laws can ultimately save a union from the domination of a determined minority that is quite unconcerned about the spirit and rules of democracy unless the average member is prepared to play some part in the government of the organisation.

What is most shocking about the current state of trade union democracy is that few observers believe that even the widespread exposure of corrupt activities or political domination by Communists will stimulate union members to assert their rights and participate actively in union affairs. It is difficult to think of any other walk of life in which a person found to be using his position to achieve ends entirely alien to the vast majority by means that violate normal ethical codes would be able to continue holding responsible office or employment. Now that the T.U.C. has found it necessary to expel the E.T.U. for refusal to comply with the directions of the General Council it will be unfortunate if this decision is not given the fullest possible support both inside and outside of the trade union movement.

The defeat of the Communists in the elections for the Executive Council is evidence that the members of the union endorse the decision of the T.U.C., but the size of the ballot – less than one-third of the members voted – indicates that the struggle to free the E.T.U. from Communist domination is by no means over.

A vital factor in tackling this problem is publicity. Union members have a right to be informed by every possible medium of communication. There is no better way of safeguarding union democracy from the corroding effects of apathy and the sinister conspiracy of Communists and any other political groups than full publicity. This is well recognised by those who stand to lose from having their activities exposed; that is why the Communists have hurled abuse at those labour reporters who have had the courage to probe their doings and reveal them to the public. No union that has nothing to hide should be afraid of publicity and critical comment from inside or outside. This is the price that must be paid by every organisation that wields power whether it be business or union, party or pressure group, public or private institution.

V

Trade Union Structure and Organisation

TRADE union membership now approaches the ten million mark. Official statistics of trade union membership were published for the first time in 1892, when there were only one and a half million members, but by 1920 trade union membership had reached eight million. In the face of economic events that proved disastrous to the level of employment, unions were unable to maintain the high peak attained. Workers left the unions more quickly than they had joined. The low point was eventually reached in 1933 when the membership stood at only half of the post-war figure. However, by 1939 a substantial recovery had been made and membership totalled six million; by the end of the Second World War the figure had been raised to eight million and three years later to almost nine and a half million. Since 1948 trade union membership has gone up only slightly; in fact, there has been a decline during the past few years from the peak reached in 1957. As yet, there is little to indicate that there is likely to be any dramatic fall in trade union membership, but this could happen if the unions do not extend their field of recruitment and the industries which have been traditionally well organised continue to shrink.

There have been considerable changes in the composition of trade union membership since before the First World War. While in 1911 the miners accounted for almost twenty-five per cent of the total number of trade unionists, today their membership amounts to little more than six per cent. The proportion of cotton textile trade unionists is also much less significant than it was in 1911. On the other hand, almost a quarter of the total now consists of members in the road transport and general labour group. But

76

perhaps the most important change is the substantial growth of the membership of the non-manual workers' unions. Trade unionism has, in fact, spread right across the spectrum of employment to include doctors, managers and technicians as well as bank and office clerks, civil servants, teachers and local government employees. There are now more than five times as many members of white-collar unions as there were before 1914. What is perhaps even more interesting is that the growth of this category of trade unionists has been steady and continuous throughout all the vicissitudes of the past forty years. Since it is likely that the numbers of workers employed in service occupations will increase and those in factory employment decrease, the trade union movement is bound to reflect this change in the composition of its membership. The effect of these changes on union policy is certain to be important since the social and political views of white-collar workers tend to be different from those of manual workers.

Number and size of unions

The number of trade unions in Britain today is just about half as many as existed at the end of the First World War. The present figure of 651 trade unions is, however, much larger than is found in many other countries. For example, in Germany 8 million trade union members are to be found in 16 industrial unions; in the United States 138 unions have between them over 17 million members.

The large number of trade unions in Britain is due to a number of factors. One of the most important has been the high value placed on autonomy and independence; with this has gone an extreme empiricism and reluctance to stick to one type as the best model to follow. Nevertheless, the number of unions dwindles steadily year by year, as amalgamations take place and old unions decide to close down.

The fall in the number of unions has continued as the number of trade union members has grown. The effect of this combination of developments has increased the average size of a British trade union over three times in the past twenty-five years. Even so, since there is even now a large number of trade unions, the average size is only 14,000 members. Total trade union membership is not distributed evenly, but is highly concentrated in a few very large organisations, two-thirds of the total membership belonging to seventeen unions each with a membership of more than a hundred thousand. At the other end of the scale there are more than 350 unions with a membership of one thousand or less.

Thus the British trade union movement consists of a small number of very large organisations and a very large number of very small organisations.*

Size is an important factor affecting the democracy and efficiency of union government and administration. Small unions generally have a higher membership participation than large ones, but they are usually less efficiently administered and cannot offer their members as comprehensive a service. It is now well recognised that the problems posed by bigness present an acute challenge to democracy. The danger is particularly great when bigness is allied to a high degree of administrative and governmental centralisation. The crucial problem is to strike the appropriate balance between centralising those things that it is essential to centralise and those that it is not. There is great need for every large-scale union to be examining its structure constantly so as to ensure that the proper balance of advantage is maintained.

Types of union

British trade union structure is further complicated by the variety of types of union and degree to which organisations overlap each other. As is well known, trade unionism began with the skilled craftsmen and only much later spread to the less skilled and non-manual workers. Thus the pattern which trade union organisation has followed, in the main, has been horizontal rather than vertical, across rather than coterminous with the boundaries of industries. Before the First World War there was a determined attempt to persuade the unions to abandon the occupational basis of their organisation in favour of organising by industry. In spite of winning the theoretical argument the industrial unionists had little practical success in converting the unions to this more logical and rational form of organisation. They greatly reduced their chance of success by linking the arguments for industrial unionism with

* For an explanation of the pattern of membership distribution see P. E. Hart and E. H. Phelps Brown, 'The Sizes of Trade Unions: A study in the Laws of Aggregation,' *The Economic Journal*, March, 1957.

the doctrine of revolutionary syndicalism. But the major defeat of industrial unionism was brought about by the remarkable success of the general unions, which had their origins in the great upsurge of unskilled labourers in the late 1880's.

The general unions of today have a very large unskilled membership, but they by no means confine their membership to one type of employee. In some industries they organise every category, including clerical and supervisory grades. Their membership is extremely diverse; the Transport and General Workers' Union has members in more than two hundred industries; the National Union of General and Municipal Workers has members in only slightly fewer industries.

Unions which were once composed entirely of apprentice-trained craftsmen have now opened their ranks to semi-skilled, unskilled and ancillary workers. The Electrical Trades Union and the Amalgamated Engineering Union, for example, have members of all grades in a wide variety of industries and they might for all practical purposes be classified as general unions.

The extraordinary feature of this development is that general unionism violates the law of common interest which the Webbs stated would prevent a trade union from extending its area of organisation beyond the boundaries of a single occupation. They were proved wrong by the instruments of representative government and of efficient full-time administration, which they themselves saw as inevitable developments. By these means unions were able to embrace diverse occupational groups and weld them into a cohesive organisation.

Closer unity

The trade unions first sought closer unity on the place of political action, and succeeded in forming a central organisation to promote and protect their wider interests in 1868. The Trades Union Congress was strictly excluded from interfering with such issues of domestic concern to the unions as were settled by collective bargaining. However, as industry developed and the unions grew larger, collective bargaining advanced from the district basis to national agreements. Since in most industries there were a large number of unions involved, the question of unity of action naturally arose. Further point was given to this question when the employers

followed the lead of the unions and formed their own organisations for the purpose of collective bargaining. The response of the
trade unions was to form industrial federations with the limited
purpose of negotiating with the employers. Most of the larger industries are now covered by federal arrangements or by national collective bargaining machinery which in effect fulfils the same
purpose.

It was thought at one time by the T.U.C. that federations would
pave the way for the amalgamation of the unions on industrial
lines. The success of the federation and the achievement of national
bargaining machinery have proved, however, to be a barrier to the
rationalisation of trade union structure, since they have enabled
unions to enjoy industry-wide bargaining without breaking up their
diverse occupation structure.

In face of their stubborn adherence to an organisational structure
that involves considerable overlapping, the unions have found it
necessary to evolve other means of settling conflicts over recruitment, bargaining rights and representation. This responsibility has
largely fallen on the T.U.C., though a number of unions now have
inter-union agreements to regulate the settlement of disputes. In
its early years the T.U.C. was extremely reluctant to take on the
role of arbiter in conflicts between its member organisations. Eventually it was compelled to assume this responsibility and it established a disputes committee and attempted to formulate what might
be described as a code of good union conduct, better known as the
Bridlington agreement, since it was adopted in that town at the
curtailed conference of 1939.

The object of the Bridlington rules is to lay down the conditions that unions should observe before recruiting new members.
Each union is called upon not to accept without an inquiry a person
who has belonged to another union. If the inquiry shows that the
member has left his previous union because he is under discipline,
while the union is engaged in a trade dispute, or that he is in
arrears with his contributions, he should not be recruited. The
appropriate questions should be included in the membership
declaration form that has to be completed on joining the union.
The agreement also states that no union should commence organising activities at any establishment in which another union has

the majority of workers and negotiates conditions, except with the agreement of that union.

What the Bridlington agreement in effect sets out to achieve is the parcelling out of jurisdictional areas on the basis of established organising rights. In other words, the rules recognise the complex character of British trade union structure and seek to consolidate it in such a way as to minimise inter-union conflict. The effect, however, of this policy, wise as it might be from the organisational point of view, is to deprive individual members of the right to join whichever union they choose. This fact was indirectly recognised by the Courts when in the case of Andrew v. National Union of Public Employees, Mr. Justice Wynn-Parry awarded an injunction to the plaintiff to restrain the union from expelling seven new members on the instruction of the T.U.C. disputes committee. The National Union of Public Employees had recruited these members without observing the Bridlington rules; following a complaint from the union which had lost the members, the T.U.C. disputes committee found on the evidence that the complaint was justified and ordered the N.U.P.E. to return the members it had wrongfully recruited. The men themselves were not, however, prepared to be drafted back, and sought the assistance of the Court, which found in their favour simply because the N.U.P.E. did not have in its rules the express power to expel a member on the instruction of the disputes committee of the T.U.C. A similar situation occurred one year later when the National Amalgamated Stevedores and Dockers' Society was restrained from expelling the 10,000 members it had 'poached' from the Transport and General Workers' Union.

The effect of the Courts' decisions in these cases was to underline the fact that an award of the T.U.C. disputes committee has no legal force, although it might well be regarded as being equitable and reasonable from the point of view of stable union organisation and good industrial relations. Of course, in the cases cited, the Courts were doing no more than strictly observing the established legal view of union rules, which is that they constitute the terms of the contract of membership. If a union wished to carry out the awards of the T.U.C. disputes committee without acting in breach of contract, it must alter its rules to this effect. Following the cases mentioned and after taking legal advice, this course was recommended by the T.U.C., and an appropriate model rule was drafted, which many unions have now adopted. Thus, in future, unions with such a rule will lawfully be able to carry out the decision of a T.U.C. disputes committee if they are found to have wrongfully recruited members and are instructed to give them back. It is obviously good sense to have machinery through which inter-union disputes may be resolved, but in the making of decisions of this kind it would be in the interests of union members if those concerned could be heard as well as the officials of the unions. Members ought not to be treated simply as if they were so many bodies.

Breakaway unions

Conflict between the rights of the individual and the needs of organisation are most acutely roused when the number of dissident members is large enough to form a new union. The right to break away and form a new union has always been condemned as calculated to undermine the strength of the parent unit, to encourage discontented members to seek a solution outside the union rather than internally through the democratic process, and to weaken the unity of the whole trade union movement.

The official policy of the T.U.C. is to refuse to affiliate a new union if there is already an existing one which organises the type of worker concerned. Even if recognition is conceded by the T.U.C., the union will not necessarily gain recognition from rival unions, the employers, or even from official institutions.

Public policy has long tended to discriminate against breakaway unions in favour of a stable unified trade union movement. During the period in which the Conditions of Employment and National Arbitration Order was in force, from 1940 to 1951, the Ministry of Labour refused to accept any report of a dispute other than from an officially recognised union. This policy was subsequently given formal recognition, when, under the Industrial Disputes Order of 1951, only unions that habitually took part in the negotiation of conditions of employment were empowered to report a dispute to the Minister. Thus a breakaway union would be deprived of the services of the Industrial Disputes Tribunal.

The formation of breakaway unions in the Civil Service has compelled the government to define its policy towards these organisations as an employer. During the period of the Labour Government there was a tendency for the Conservatives in opposition to favour the support of breakaway unions, but in office they have followed the same policy as their predecessors. In deciding to do this they were able to rely on the report of a special committee (under the chairmanship of Lord Terrington, chairman of the Industrial Disputes Tribunal) appointed to consider the problem* in the Post Office. The conclusions of the Terrington Committee were (1) that it was undesirable to have more than one union representing the same grade of worker; (2) that an association claiming recognition should be required to prove that existing associations had failed and were unable to look after the interests of the workers concerned. Thus the position which now prevails in the Civil Service is that the government will not recognise for bargaining purposes any new union unless it can survive these tests, which are, as experience has proved, almost impossible to meet.

Those who have studied the problem are well aware of the acute dilemma this issue poses, and opinions may differ as to the wisdom of the decision of the government. I think that it was in the best interests of good industrial relations, the unions and their members. It is only under conditions of reasonable security that unions can develop liberal and sensible policies. If they are constantly afraid that they are going to be undermined by hostile employers and dissident members they will inevitably seek at all costs to prevent such events from materialising; they will behave in a rigid and ruthless fashion in order to safeguard their existence. Nevertheless, it must also be recognised that in certain circumstances it might be necessary to repudiate unrepresentative leadership by wholesale desertion and the formation of a new union. When such situations arise it would be stupid of the employers, the T.U.C. and the government to stick woodenly to their general attitude of non-encouragement.

While stressing the need to respect the rights of workers to join unions of their own choice it is also necessary to emphasise the need to rationalise the structure of the unions. The T.U.C. has itself indicated how best this might be done. Unfortunately it has not followed up its *Report on Structure and Closer Unity*, made fifteen years ago, with the vigour and determination required. As a minimum objective it should at least seek to achieve the objectives of that report within the next five years. It is surely a disgrace to

* Post Office (Departmental Classes) Recognition Committee, Cmd. 8470.

modern trade unionism that serious stoppages of work should be allowed to take place over such questions as 'demarcation'; these could be prevented by resolute leadership.

Freedom of association

Everybody in Britain over the age of sixteen is, in law, with one exception, free to join or not to join a trade union. Only members of the police forces are prevented, by the Police Act, 1919, from freely joining a trade union or any other association which seeks to negotiate salaries, pensions or conditions of service, unless they were members at the time they joined the service and they receive the permission of their chief officer to remain members; but they must not engage in any activities that could lead to a breach of discipline.

Freedom to join a trade union does not mean that a person has any legal right to insist on a union admitting him to membership. Unions are legally entitled to limit their membership according to any principle which they choose. It is possible to envisage circumstances in which unions discriminate against certain groups and by so doing deprive them of the right to work. If discrimination is carried to those lengths and it has adverse consequences for those denied entry, there is a case for legal regulation, and this will be considered, along with other aspects of the 'closed shop', in the next section.

Employers are equally free in Britain to make union membership or non-membership a condition of employment. There are quite a few firms which have no union members among their employees, but there are very few which make non-union membership a condition of employment. One such firm, D. C. Thomson Ltd., of Dundee, was involved in a fierce battle with the trade unions in the printing industry a few years ago when it was revealed that many employees had actually joined a union. No one could make Thomsons change their policy and not even an appeal from Mr. Churchill, who was then Prime Minister, could persuade them to recognise the unions.

In the United States any attempt by an employer to interfere with the right of one of his employees to join a union is illegal, and refusal to bargain with a union that has been certified by the National Labour Relations Board is an offence. British unions have never asked for such legal assistance, since they have realised that to do so would be to invite legal control over their affairs to a far greater extent than they would desire. The more important problem in recent times has been not the making of non-unionism but the making of unionism a condition of employment.

To make union membership a condition of employment is perfectly respectable at law. In the Crofter case, the House of Lords upheld the right of a trade union to use its bargaining strength to achieve a situation in which workers would have to be members of the union.* It is difficult to say how widespread compulsory unionism is today, but the areas of industry in which it prevails are limited.†

Compulsory unionism

It is necessary to distinguish two different types of compulsory unionism, since from the point of view of the union and of management there is an important difference between them. The 'closed shop' in its proper sense means that no person may be employed who does not hold a union card, and the union concerned is, therefore, able to determine the supply of labour. This situation is extremely rare, though it does exist in sections of some industries. The T.U.C. is not in favour of the full 'closed shop', since it gives one union complete jurisdiction and this raises difficulties when union boundaries so often overlap. The goal which the T.U.C. supports is 100 per cent trade unionism; that is to say, it believes that every employee ought to belong to a trade union, but not necessarily to one particular organisation. This may seem to many readers like splitting hairs, but it is typical of British industrial relations; it lets the T.U.C. out of a difficult position without abandoning the main objective, which is to get everybody into a union.

The advantages of compulsory membership to unions and to management are fairly obvious. When everybody has automatically to be a member, a union can rely upon a steady membership and regular income, and it can concentrate on improving its government, administration and service to members. Management gains the advantage of not being caught in the crossfire of an organisa-

---

* *Crofter Hand Woven Harris Tweed Co. v Veitch* (1942), A.C. 435.
† For a detailed analysis of the present situation see my *Trade Union Government & Administration in Great Britain*, Ch. 2.

tional struggle. Responsibility is more clearly pinned upon the union and greater co-operation can be expected. The one who stands to gain least is the member of the union. Indeed, the most powerful argument against compulsory unionism is that it removes the last important safeguard of the member, the right to drop out when he feels like it. Experience in America and elsewhere has shown that compulsory unionism is a potent factor in the decay of union democracy; its effects are insidious and difficult to combat. It is for these reasons that the extension of compulsory unionism should be resisted in spite of its advantage to unions and management.

Compulsory unionism has recently been brought into the forefront of public discussion by a series of legal cases involving the expulsion of union members. When union membership is purely voluntary and there is more than one organisation to which a man may belong, it perhaps does not matter too much if a member is expelled since he can always join another organisation. If, however, his expulsion means loss of his job and he cannot easily get another because the union has a widespread 'closed shop', it raises the gravest issues of public policy.

These issues were raised in the Bonsor case a few years ago, and they are so important that it is worth while considering them in detail. Bonsor was a musician who was in arrears with his contributions and, by all accounts, he was not a very good trade unionist. After being out of work Bonsor was offered a post in an orchestra, but could not start his employment without a 'clean card'. When he offered to pay his arrears out of his first week's wages Bonsor was refused by his branch secretary, who told him he had been expelled from the union. Bonsor asked the Courts to declare that he had been wrongfully expelled and to give him damages for loss incurred as a result of the breach of contract. The Courts ultimately found, on the facts of the case, that he had been wrongfully expelled, since the secretary had not the power to take this step under the rules, and that he was entitled to damages.

This case was important because it established beyond a shadow of doubt that the Courts will do their utmost to protect a member from the might of an organisation. The union must act strictly in conformity with the rules, otherwise an action may lie against it. This is to the good, since the rules are there to protect the member, and it is right that union officials should be aware that they may cost their organisation thousands of pounds in legal costs and damages if they do not behave correctly. But supposing the union had drawn its rules in such a way as to try to exclude the jurisdiction of the Courts?

It is almost certain that rules which suggest, as they do in some cases, that the decision of the union shall be final and binding and that under no circumstances shall the member initiate legal proceedings in respect of any matter that arises out of an interpretation of the rules would be regarded as an attempt to oust the jurisdiction of the Courts on a matter of law. Should the union go even farther and try to exclude its rules entirely from the purview of the Courts by making them binding in honour only, it is almost certain that the Courts would declare such an attempt as contrary to public policy and therefore void. The Courts would, it is believed by authorities, equally certainly strike down as contrary to public policy any attempt to give the leaders of the union arbitrary powers to expel that would violate the principles of 'natural justice'. Thus, the trend of judicial opinion is clearly moving strongly in favour of the individual as the Courts exercise their classic function of protecting the weaker party from the tyranny of the stronger.

It cannot be too strongly emphasised that it is a first requirement of domestic trade unionism that the rules should be properly drawn so as to ensure that the rights of members are adequately protected. It has been suggested by a group of Conservative lawyers that the Registrar of Friendly Societies ought to be directed to refuse to register a union if its rules do not conform to certain standards.* Whilst one may not be able to endorse all the suggestions made by this group, it certainly has a strong case for its proposal that no union should be registered if it did not adopt rules to protect its members from expulsion or over-drastic punishment for offences, and to provide for any dispute between a member and a union being decided in a fair manner.

* *A Giant's Strength,* a Study by the Inns of Court Conservative and Unionist Society.

The most perfect of rules will not in themselves guarantee that members may not find themselves victims of arbitrary decisions. We have seen that the Courts will defend the member against violation of his rights, but it would not be in the interests of good trade unionism to encourage members to litigate every time they had a grievance. It would be more in keeping with the autonomous character of British trade unionism if they contributed to a solution of these problems by establishing their own appeals tribunals on the lines suggested earlier.*

Trade union leadership

So far we have been concerned with the constitutional aspects of union democracy as they affect the right of workers to join unions and the right of workers not to be expelled arbitrarily. Protection of the interests of the member will depend, however, to a great extent on the quality of the leadership rather than on the union's rules. We have discussed the effect of politics on union leadership, but this is not the only factor that affects the behaviour of union leaders.

Senior union leaders are usually men of strong character and personality who have climbed to the top of the ladder by dint of struggle, determination and ability. Once they reach the top of big unions they become important national figures, called upon to participate in a wide variety of activities which to the ordinary member sometimes seem remote from his interests.

This development is an inevitable by-product of the rise in the status of the unions. When, however, general secretaries sit on many committees and Royal Commissions, travel overseas on international delegations, and at the same time are responsible for the affairs of a large-scale business, they tend to be overworked. The net effect is that sometimes little time is available for dealing with the internal affairs of their own unions. Pressing problems are, of course, dealt with, and when the occasion requires it other things are put off to ensure that the union's interests are looked after. The round of activities is so great that once a man becomes a general secretary he rarely gets a moment to reflect, to sit back and study the problems of his organisation and the issues that confront it. This situation would not be so bad if there was a tradition of

* See Chapter IV, page 74.

devolution of authority and responsibility in British unions. Unfortunately this is not the case; indeed, the tendency has been in the other direction, that is, for the process of decision-making to become more centralised and mount higher up the pyramid of authority. All this means that the load of responsibility carried by the senior officer of a British trade union is really immense.

Two things are required by British trade union leadership fairly urgently: one is devolution of authority, and the other is more expert assistance. These two things are, in fact, closely related and cannot really be separated.

Some general secretaries have personal assistants who are invaluable, but too often they are faithful old general office employees who are steeped in conservatism. They tend to be an obstacle rather than a stimulant to imaginative developments. There are some instances of British trade union leaders having the assistance of a really able administrative officer and a reasonable research department, but these are in a distinct minority of cases. Readers will no doubt be tired of having Mr. Walter Reuther cited as an example; unfortunately it is difficult to find another union leader who has pioneered in so many fields. In this case no British union can match the brilliant team of executive officers whom Mr. Reuther has gathered round him. It is the function of this group to think out and develop the ideas which the U.A.W. has put into practice with such remarkable success.

Most British unions are understaffed by comparison with American, German or Russian trade unions. If better services are to be provided, if closer communications with members are to be achieved, then it is imperative that the number of paid officials should be increased. To provide more staff and more experts at national level who are capable of servicing the active officers of the union is a costly business. It cannot be done without spending much more money on administration than has been the case in the past. The problem is not merely that of spending more on salaries, since more employees will mean more office space, more equipment, more expenses for many other items.

Trade union finance

Any suggestion that unions should spend more money immediately produces long faces and worried frowns. The trade unions are not as well off as they at first sight appear to be, and money is at bottom the key to many improvements that could be desired in trade union organisation. Altogether registered trade unions have reserve funds amounting to £86 million. This sum is not large when it is divided by the membership, and is measured in terms of funds per head. In 1959 it was £10; this compares with the pre-war figure of £3 16s. 1d. in 1936.

The financial strength of the unions was revealed by the bus strike of 1958. This strike, which involved only some 50,000 workers, is said to have cost the union £1,600,000. The drain on the union's funds was such that it asked the T.U.C. to appeal to all the other unions for financial aid on its behalf, and it solicited interest-free loans.

The Transport and General Workers' Union was reduced to seeking aid from other organisations for several reasons which exemplify the problem that faces many other unions. Although at the commencement of the bus strike it had total funds of over £11 million, a large proportion of this amount was not in easily realisable assets. A substantial amount (in 1956 more than 50 per cent) was invested in British government securities. Much of this stock had been purchased when consols and public utilities were standing at much higher levels than today, and to sell would have involved the union in a considerable capital loss of about £1½ million. Most British trade unions are in the same boat in this respect. Although they are quite free to invest in industrial equities, so long as they take the appropriate powers, they have not done so for ideological reasons. As investors of their members' funds, unions have behaved as conservatively as the most crusted of charity trustees. A more harsh, but not entirely unjustified criticism, would be to suggest that the unions have negligently allowed their members' assets to be eaten up by inflation, since they could, by a more intelligent investment policy, have done more to safeguard their real value. Many observers from the City of London must have found the sight of a union appealing for help, rather than sell government securities at a loss, a piquant spectacle. In the past two years certain unions have made arrangements to put some of their funds in equities through a unit trust.

Nevertheless, in spite of a rather uninspired record as investors, the income from investments has saved a large number of unions from being in the red for a number of years. Not very long ago the T.U.C. found that nearly fifty unions spent more in 1954 than they had received in contributions that year. In actual cash, allowing for the fall in the value of money, unions in 1954 were able to set aside for the future from contributions less than one-sixth of the amount they were putting to reserve in 1939.* This was due to the fact that spending on administration in 1954 was about three times as high as it had been in 1939. During these years membership had risen by 50 per cent; but the costs of administration per member went up by 80 per cent. Most significant of all, contributions were up by about 25 per cent, on average, whereas earnings had risen 300 per cent. The annual report of the Registrar of Friendly Societies, relating to trade unions in 1959, shows that the situation is, if anything, getting worse rather than better.†

The bald truth of the matter is that British workers get their trade unionism on the cheap; in no other country in the world are union contributions, as a proportion of earnings, so low. Had they been fixed at, say, 1 per cent of the weekly wage, as they are in some countries, or at the value of an hour's work, contributions would have risen automatically and the unions would not have found themselves in financial difficulties. It might, of course, be thought that the unions have all the money that they require if they do not follow a strike policy, and that larger funds would only encourage the hotter heads to greater irresponsibility.

It must be admitted that the existence of large funds does attract the attention of the belligerently inclined – but on the other hand, as we have seen on many occasions, union leaders never like to see their funds dissipated no matter how big they may be. It is not, however, larger funds that are required, but a larger income and expenditure on those items that would make the unions more efficient instruments and more capable of playing a constructive role in the modern world.

* T.U.C. Annual Report, 1956.
† *Report of the Chief Registrar of Friendly Societies for the year 1959, Part 4, Trade Unions.*

Higher contributions may have another incidental benefit. They might well persuade members to take a more active interest in the affairs of the unions and the way in which they are governed. Nothing adds interest to the way in which an organisation is being conducted more than the knowledge that one's own money is involved.

VI

Summary of Conclusions

1. Trade unions are vitally important institutions in a free society, since they serve as an instrument of democratic self-government. Their right to protect and promote the interests of their members should never be superseded by the state. It is a function of the state to see that a proper balance between the interests of different sections of the community is maintained, but the primary responsibility for ensuring that the power which collective organisation confers is not abused rests with the unions and employers themselves.

2. Unions should not seek to push up wages at a rate that is faster than the increase in output and they should be prepared to accept measures required to prevent inflation. These would involve a more reasonable definition of full employment than an excess of jobs over persons available to fill them. More attention should be given to fringe benefits and long-term agreements.

3. The structure of collective bargaining should be changed where necessary to allow for more local agreements and more attention to plant problems.

4. Restrictive practices cannot be eradicated by legal process. They can only be eliminated by first-class management and constructive trade unionism.

5. Compulsory arbitration is not a solution to the problem of strikes, nor is the compulsory ballot. The right to strike should not be curtailed, but the government has a duty to protect the public

from the adverse effects of strikes so far as this is possible. There is a need to deal with unofficial strikes by more comprehensive definition of the contract of employment and the development of a system of grievance arbitration. Careful consideration ought to be given by employers' organisations and trade unions to the advantages to be gained from making collective agreements into collective contracts.

6. Unions should exercise more effective control over shop stewards by integrating them more closely with the structure of the union.

7. Joint consultative committees are not a substitute for good management; more emphasis should be given to raising the standards of management, supervision and day-to-day consultation.

8. There is a need to bring union politics into the open. Members are entitled to know the politics of union candidates, and present rules, which often prevent this information from being passed on, are not in the best interests of democracy.

9. The law should be changed so as to limit the legal privileges of unions to registered organisations. Registration should only be granted to organisations which in their rules, satisfy the requirements of 'natural justice' and protect the rights of members. The Registrar should also be given power to investigate complaints of violations of general rules; and to enforce their observance in the same way as he may now do in connexion with the political fund rules of unions. The Minister of Labour should also be empowered to appoint a fact-finding Court of Inquiry on the recommendation of the Registrar. But unions ought to take their own steps to protect the interests of members by establishing the right of appeal to an outside committee.

10. Union membership ought not to be made a condition of employment, since this violates the rights of the individual and removes an essential safeguard against the abuse of power.

11. Public policy should not encourage 'breakaway' unions, since this is not in the interests of good trade unionism or sound indus-

trial relations. But the T.U.C. ought to take far more vigorous action to bring about a reform of trade union structure along the lines proposed in the *Report on Structure and Closer Unity*. Demarcation disputes ought to be prevented by changes in union structure and more resolute leadership.

12. There is a need to improve the quality of union leadership by provision of more assistance and ancillary services.

13. Trade union subscriptions should be raised and union funds more efficiently managed.

PART TWO

Unions in the U.S.A.

I

Introduction

THE organisation of labour has a long history in America. Trade unionism is, in fact, older than the United States, since its origins may be traced back to colonial days. In most countries trade unionism is now a normal part of the social scene, but only in Britain does it have earlier beginnings than in the United States.

The right of working people to organise, to protect and advance their vocational interests, to bargain collectively, and, if necessary, to go on strike is now well established in custom and in law in America. But it was not always so, and there are still those who vigorously challenge the right of the unions to exist and who would deny them the opportunity of carrying out their activities on behalf of their members. In most parts of America these outright opponents of trade unionism are in a distinct minority, but in some areas they exercise a dominant political influence and unions are kept at bay by ruthless methods. Of far greater significance, however, is the fact that, in spite of the long history of trade unionism, a large section of the community is uneasy, worried, and apprehensive about the contemporary and future role of labour organisations.

It is not surprising that unions evoke criticism and hostility from those who own, manage, and provide professional services to industry, since unions present a constant challenge to their authority and status. The organisation of labour and the evolution of collective bargaining have inevitably limited the power of management to make untrammelled decisions. Over a large section of industry the activities of trade unions have resulted in the development of a system of law and order that enables the employee to enjoy a degree of job security and justice that is guaranteed by collective contract instead of resting on the personal whim and caprice of foreman or manager. This must be reckoned a tremendous gain for democracy in any community, and it has been recognised as such by the legislative Acts of the United States' Congress.

These developments, though naturally disliked by those whose power has been restricted, have been widely accepted as an essential feature of a modern society. They have been recognised as a vital part of the development of the contemporary system of democracy which has been variously described as pluralism, contingent anarchy, or the system of countervailing power. Under this method of ordering our social affairs, no single institution can be the repository of total power: authority is subdivided and decentralised among and within many different independent organisations. Each institution is a counterpoise to the rest, including the state itself. It is, therefore, of fundamental importance that the balance of force should not be disturbed by any institution becoming so powerful as to dominate the remainder, or so undemocratic, corrupt, and irresponsible as to jeopardise the fundamental liberties of any person and undermine the progress and stability of the economy.

Here, then, we come to the essence of the problem. It is suggested, on the one hand, that unions have now grown so strong that they do exercise undue power and influence over industry and government. Another set of critics, on the other hand, asserts that the trade union movement appears to have already passed the zenith of its development, that it is now in a state of stagnation from which it is unlikely to escape.*

What, then, will the future of the American labour movement be? Has the membership of the unions reached a plateau? What are the prospects for further growth? Are they as hopeless as some observers seem to think?

Much attention has been paid recently to the alleged undemocratic character of American unions. It has been pointed out that as organisations grow larger, their leadership becomes more professionalised, and the making of decisions is increasingly centralised, local unionism is gradually being left functionless. Is this an inevitable development, or can it be prevented?

The investigations of the Senate Committee on Improper Activi-

* R. A. Lester, *As Unions Mature*, Princeton University Press, Princeton, 1958.

ties in the Labour or Management Field revealed to the public
the extent to which, in some unions, leaders have violated democratic procedures and corruptly helped themselves to union funds
on a staggering scale. Are these features of the American labour
movement unfortunate aberrations, or do they represent a general
trend towards a moral degeneration that arises out of the very
nature of trade unionism? Can the trade unions put their house in
order? Will the AFL-CIO ethical codes prove effective against
the defiance of union leaders determined to ignore them? The
Labour Management Reporting and Disclosure Act is designed to
protect the rights of union members and to save them from the
predatory activities of unscrupulous officials; will this legislation
succeed in accomplishing the intentions of its authors?

The persistent tendency for prices to rise in the post-war years
is cited as evidence that the unions have become too big and too
powerful and are responsible for pushing up wages faster than can
be absorbed by the rate of economic expansion.* Is the process
of collective bargaining bound to produce inflationary consequences
in conditions of full employment? What is the cost of achieving
price stability?

The contributions of the unions to the political funds of the
Democratic Party, the lending of organising assistance in political
campaigns, and the constant pressure of union lobbyists on state
and federal congressmen constitute, it is suggested, a serious threat
to the free exercise of the powers of government. In other words,
it is feared, in some quarters, that the strength of the unions has
now become so great as to constitute a menace to the well-being
of society as a whole. It is, therefore, felt by business men to be
imperative that steps should be taken to curb the over-mighty
power of the unions and so restore the desirable balance of authority
in the community.

These are the contemporary issues that are posed by trade unions
in America today. They are issues that are not confined to the
United States; most of them, in one form or another, have been
raised in Britain and other European countries. It is interesting,
therefore, to compare the trends of development in the United
States with those apparent in Britain.

* Edward H. Chamberlin, 'Labour Union Power and the Public Interest',
The Public Stake in Union Power, University of Virginia Press, 1959.

When comparing trade union developments in the United States with those in Britain it is necessary to remember certain historical and background factors that go far to explain some of the differences that are apparent. These factors have been responsible for some attractive and some unattractive features of the contemporary American labour movement.

The first and most obvious difference is that America is a very large country. Distance and physical obstacles made communication difficult until relatively modern times and separated one area from another. Climate and the time and extent of settlement made for vast differences in the character of the East, South, Mid-West, South-West, Rocky Mountains, and Pacific Coast regions of the United States. The trade union movement grew up and spread over an area as vast and as varied as that which extends from Spain to the Ukraine. Given such geographical conditions the emphasis on local autonomy was bound to be strong.

The need to acknowledge local differences and the difficulty of governing such a huge and diverse area from a single capital was recognised in the constitution of the United States. Law was a matter for the states as well as the Federal Government. There could be and there were, and there still are today, considerable differences in the laws passed by the states to regulate the activities of trade unions. Labour organisations had to deal not with one government, as in Britain, but with many; an activity that might be legal in one state could be unlawful in another.

In their early days unions in America had to face the hostility of the Courts, which, following British tradition, were antipathetic to collective organisations that acted in restraint of trade. The unions were supported, however, by the powerful tide of Jacksonian democracy which pounded against the class-inspired notions of the Courts, and a society dominated by an aspiring, superior, if not aristocratic, upper stratum of wealthy farmers, merchants and manufacturers. By 1842, under the influence of a strong current of egalitarianism, the Courts had freed the American unions from actions based on the English doctrine of conspiracy.* American workers had enjoyed the right to vote for at least a generation before it was conceded to their British cousins. At the time the Chartists were pressing for the reform of Parliament, American

*Commonwealth v Hunt, Massachusetts Supreme Court, 1842.

workers had their own parties in New York and other eastern states, and vigorously engaged in political agitation for economic and social reforms. Again and again in the nineteenth century unions in America were lured into political movements by the influence of Utopian reformers, but these ventures were rarely profitable.

Convinced that constant diversion from the task of building and consolidating their organisation was disastrous for the unions, Samuel Gompers, the founder of the American Federation of Labour, determined to keep them free of party political ties. The unions ought to shun any attempt to identify themselves with an ideology; their political philosophy should be limited to 'rewarding their friends and punishing their enemies'. Previous experience persuaded American workers that Gompers was right and the trade union movement began to develop on strict bread-and-butter craft unionist principles. Events were eventually to stimulate the unions into taking a more active interest in politics, but to this day they have refused to follow the example of the British unions and form a political party of their own. Instead they have continued to support Gompers's dictum, but they have drawn close to the Democratic Party as a matter of practical expediency likely to yield the greatest return, rather than as a matter of ideological principle.

By contrast with Britain, which is an old, settled country with an homogenous population tightly packed on a small island, America is a new country, its population having grown rapidly by means of immigration from every country in Europe. As new immigrants arrived and the population grew, it spread west until the frontier was the Pacific Ocean. The immigrant waves made trade union organisation difficult. Most of the newcomers arrived with nothing but the ability to work. Many of them did not speak English. They had to find jobs and they were easily exploited until they had put down roots and established themselves. But in spite of the vast influx, demand for labour soon overtook supply and high wages were easily obtained without the need for unions.

Trade unionism grew among the skilled craftsmen settled in the older cities of the eastern seaboard states. When the unskilled and newer workers lost their jobs or had a row with the boss it was as easy for them to move on westward as to stay and fight for an improvement of their lot by joining a trade union.

An idea of the problem that wave after wave of immigration brought for the American trade unions can be vividly realised by the simple fact that the United Mineworkers' Union has put out its bulletins in more than a score of different languages. No British trade union ever faced an organising problem similar to the one that beset many American unions.

Until the breathtaking momentum of the colonisation of the North American continent slowed down, there was little possibility of the trade unions consolidating their organisation as they did in Britain in the fifty years that came after 1875. The rapid growth of America, the federal structure of government, the heterogenous character of the population, made law-breaking common and law enforcement difficult. America was born out of an act of defiance of the law, and Americans have been constantly faced with the problem of imposing law on a society that has a tradition of its members making their own law. The right to carry arms to defend one's life and property is still regarded as a fundamental right; the frontier with its lawlessness perpetuated the tradition that men had a right to take the law into their own hands. It is perhaps for this reason that the history of American trade unionism is more full of violence, bloodshed and every kind of intimidation than any other labour movement. The unions were at times fought by every means, legal and illegal, and they hit back at employers with similar ruthless methods whenever they had the opportunity.

It was not the fierce opposition of employers that threatened the existence of the American trade unions so much as great economic depression which followed the Wall Street crash of 1929, and the tired leadership of the American Federation of Labour, which failed to adjust its ideas to the needs of the workers in America's modern mass-production industries. It was the election of President Roosevelt and his New Deal that put new life into a moribund trade union movement and laid the basis of the National Labour Relations Act, which gave the trade unions a privileged position in the community for the great advance to their present status.

The legislation of the New Deal period and much that has followed has been to a greater or lesser extent in conflict with the tradition established by the Sherman anti-trust Act of promoting competition. After 1892 the Sherman Act was used against the unions as well as business organisations until they were specifically excluded from anti-trust injunctions by the Clayton Act of 1914. Anti-trust laws do, however, have an important effect on collective bargaining, since they promote competition between employers and deter the development of industry-wide bargaining. When suggestions were made recently that the motor companies might enter into a profit-sharing arrangement to resist the pressure of the union brought to bear against one of them, it was at once claimed by the union leaders that this action would be a violation of the anti-trust laws.

America has enjoyed much more aggressive competition, a much higher rate of economic growth and much higher wages than Britain during this century. The character of the trade union movement and the quality of industrial relations in America have been much influenced by these facts. There is evidence of a slowing down in the tempo of life in America, competition is rather less fierce, and there seems to be a growing expectation that the government will have a more rather than a less significant role to play in the future. The change in mood and direction will inevitably influence the course of relations in industry in the future.

II

The Structure of Union Organisation

LESS than one out of every three workers eligible to join trade unions is a member of a labour organisation in the United States. By comparison with Britain where the proportion is almost one out of every two, or Sweden where the proportion is three out of every four, the density of trade union organisation is relatively low in America. But there has been a startling change during the past quarter of a century, with developments in the United States outpacing the European countries. In 1932 only one in twelve employees belonged to a trade union; in the intervening twenty-five years trade union membership increased by 15 million, or about fivefold. By comparison, union membership in Britain only trebled.

The foundation of the great surge forward in trade union membership was laid during the early days of the New Deal and consolidated with the passing of the National Labour Relations Act in 1935. The basic purpose of this Act was to protect the unions from the attacks of employers by making it an unfair labour practice for any employer to interfere with the right of an employee to join and participate in the activities of a union, to refuse to recognise and bargain in good faith with a union. To ensure that the Act was carried out, a National Labour Relations Board was established with power to certify, after a representative election, a union as a lawful bargaining agent. The National Labour Relations Act provided a degree of legal protection to trade unions and an encouragement to their growth that went far beyond anything ever contemplated by trade unionists in Britain. In 1947 an amending Act, popularly known as the Taft-Hartley Act, was passed which represented a change of attitude towards the unions.

It was now feared that the unions were becoming over-mighty, and the law was amended to protect employers from the unfair labour practices of unions. Among a number of changes the closed shop was made illegal and employers were permitted to reply to union propaganda. Employers welcomed the Taft-Hartley Act but, though it retained the fundamental protection of union rights, it was hated by organised labour.

Had the gains in trade union membership made in the years of recovery after the 'great depression' and during the Second World War continued after 1945 at the same pace, the United States would have caught up with the older countries. But during the past decade the rate of increase has slowed down to almost a stop. It now begins to look as if a plateau has been reached, and before new heights can be scaled a major break-through into new areas of recruitment will be required.

The slowing down of the rate of increase in union membership to little better than a standstill is also a feature of the European trade union movement. There is, however, this significant difference: the slow-down in Britain, and elsewhere, came after a much higher proportion of employees had been organised.

Trade unionism in the United States has not spread to any significant extent beyond the boundaries of the 'blue-collar workers'. This fact presents a challenge to the unions of tremendous significance, since the pattern of industrial employment is one in which the proportion of 'blue-' to 'white-collar' workers steadily declines.

Of the 55 million employees in the United States, only 25 million are to be found in those categories of employment from which the unions have traditionally drawn their members, namely craftsmen, operatives, and labourers. In the decade after 1947, the number of clerical employees increased by 23 per cent; the number of professional and technical employees by no less than 60 per cent. But during the same period the numbers of factory workers and labourers increased by little over 4 per cent.

This kind of trend is not confined to America. It is taking place in all the highly industrialised countries. In Britain, for example, during the decade 1948–58, administrative, technical and clerical staff increased from 16 per cent of the total work force employed in manufacturing industry to 21 per cent. If this rate of increase continues the proportion of employees in these groups will be larger than that of manual workers well before the end of this century.*

As industry advances along the road of automation fewer people will be employed on traditional manufacturing operations. More and more goods will be produced by fewer and fewer workers employed directly on the production process. Many more clerks will be required to do the planning, checking, and recording. There will be a larger need for technicians, designers, engineers, and controllers. What is sometimes referred to as Parkinson's Law† is in fact the inevitable outcome of the growing complexity of a technological civilisation. As society becomes increasingly affluent larger numbers will be employed in the service trades and the consumer and recreation industries.

The changing character of the structure of employment is bound to have a profound effect on the trade union movement. If the unions are not to decline in importance they will have to organise the rapidly expanding areas of employment which at present are largely outside their competence. It has been estimated that about 85 per cent of the 18 million workers who belong to unions in America hold blue-collar jobs; only minor inroads have been made into the vast area of white-collar occupations.

What are the chances that the American trade union movement will be able to break through the present bounds of organisation? This question is by no means easy to answer, since there are grounds for arriving at entirely opposite conclusions.

Although the American unions, with certain exceptions, have not been very successful in organising workers in the white-collar groups, unions in other countries have had more success. In Britain over 20 per cent of the total number of trade unionists, in a proportionately much larger trade union movement, are in the ranks of the white-collar workers, and this proportion is rising. The Scandinavian countries, Germany, and Austria have had even more success. In the less well-developed countries, white-collar workers have been among the most strongly organised.

In Asia, Africa, the West Indies, and other countries where trade unionism is a very modern phenomenon, organisation did not take root first among skilled craftsmen because these societies had no

* See *Ministry of Labour Gazette,* July, 1959.
† C. Northcote Parkinson, *Parkinson's Law,* John Murray, 1958.

industry to speak of. The working population consisted mainly of peasant farmers and their families rather than industrial workers.

The only groups that were capable of forming organisations were the teachers and government clerks and the railway and port transport workers. These were the people who had settled employment, an employer to negotiate with, and issues to bargain about. They were also people who had, through education and experience, acquired the social skills necessary to form continuous associations for the purpose of collective action. It was from the white-collar groups that leaders were found who were able to spread the idea of trade unionism to plantation, service, and commercial employees.

Past experience of union growth certainly suggests that caution should be exercised before arriving at the conclusion that particular groups or classes of working-people are not organisable. It was vehemently asserted in Britain during the nineteenth century that the unskilled workers would never be organised, and similar sentiments were uttered in America as late as the 1930's. The Webbs, for example, after an exhaustive survey of trade union history were sceptical of the possibility of organising on any other basis but craft unionism. They were proved wrong almost before their book was published.

A factor which has undoubtedly played an important part in encouraging white-collar workers to join unions in Britain has been the narrowing of wage and salary differentials in favour of blue-collar workers. The growth of massive industrial enterprises, especially in the public field, has also contributed. 'This organisation is so big,' confided an engineer to the author not long ago, 'that one needs a union to keep an eye on what is going on that might, sometime in the future, affect your interests.'

So far these factors do not appear to have had a major impact on the attitudes of American white-collar workers. This could be for two reasons: either white-collar workers are especially well integrated into the structure of modern enterprise and their problems are effectively taken care of by the companies that employ them, or the unions have failed to recognise that they are different from blue-collar workers and cannot simply be treated as if they were the same.

There is good reason to think that there are many stresses and strains among the different groups of white-collar workers, and that not all of them are by any means satisfied with their status, rewards, and sense of purpose. They might not yet all be described as ripe for organisation, but important groups affected by rapid technological change might be induced to seek organisation to protect their interests. Unions are not likely to secure their allegiance, however, so long as they consider white-collar employees to be simply blue-collar employees with bleached shirts. Administrative, technical and clerical employees often look on union policy and tactics in quite a different way from manual workers.

The problem which faces the American unions is in many respects similar to that of the 1930's, when the craft unions refused to recognise that they had to employ new techniques and to change their structure if they were to recruit the operatives and labourers employed in the mass-production industries. To organise the white-collar workers may well involve the establishment of new unions, even perhaps a new central body. This is the situation in Sweden and Germany, where the white-collar unions are affiliated with a separate national federation, and this fact is an important element in the degree to which white-collar workers are organised. The separation of white-collar unions is a recognition of the social structure in these countries, which places clerical and professional employees in a different category from manual workers. White-collar workers in Europe generally do not want to take part in strikes; they do not want to feel that their future is determined by men who work principally with their hands instead of with their brains. They are different from blue-collar employees: they speak a different language, have different views and opinions and, if they join a union, want to join one that manifestly recognises these facts. Although it might appear to be contrary to the concepts of egalitarianism that are cherished in America, there is some reason to believe, from their behaviour, that white-collar workers on that side of the Atlantic share the outlook of their European opposite numbers. This means that it may be necessary to develop a new type of organisation that is part union, part professional association.

The unions show some signs of recognising the significance of these factors, but when they do they are reluctant to face the implications. In an extremely interesting speech to the Professional, Technical and Salary Conference Board of the International Union of Electrical, Radio and Machine Workers, AFL-CIO, given in

June, 1958, Everett M. Kassalow, Research Director of the Industrial Union Department, AFL-CIO, dwelt on these problems. Mr. Kassalow emphasised that, in his opinion, the unions were once again confronted with the job of adapting their organisation and structure with sufficient imagination to bring the white-collar and professional workers within their fold. However, after noting that in Europe the professional needs of these groups were met more easily because they were organised in separate engineering, technical, and clerical unions, Mr. Kassalow expressed the opinion that:

'in the United States it will not be possible to choose the road of building separate professional and technical unions for many of these workers. Economic power in America, to a considerable extent, flows along corporate and industrial lines. If white-collar, professional and technical workers are to be effectively organised, they must somehow be grouped together in the great institution which industrial workers have already established to offset the great centres of corporate power – namely the powerful industrial unions in steel, auto, rubber, oil, textile and other fields.'

It would have been difficult for Mr. Kassalow to utter any other opinion, though in fairness it must be said that he concluded with the statement that it would be necessary to strengthen the white-collar and professional unions representing workers outside the basic industries and large corporations. He also indicated that several AFL-CIO affiliates had already succeeded in organising large numbers of white-collar and professional workers. For example, the Communication Workers of America, the Airline Pilots, and the American Radio Association had all broken through the boundaries of resistance to union organisation. If they could win the allegiance of employees, similar results could be achieved elsewhere.

The success of these organisations underlined the weakness, up to now, of the industrial union approach to this problem. If the unions are going to insist on organising white-collar, technical, and professional workers within industrial unions, without paying special regard to their needs, they will almost certainly fail as lamentably as did the craft unions in the 1930's.

The ultimate factor which will eventually determine whether these groups become organised will be the extent to which they feel that they require organisation to cushion the impact of employmental pressures upon them. If technological developments continue to generate an ever-increasing burden of tensions, individual frustration, and group disintegration, salvation is bound to be sought through organisation. The genuine satisfaction of the needs of these groups is, then, the challenge which faces both employers and trade unions. Its outcome is bound to influence profoundly the future course of trade unionism, industrial relations, and the wider aspects of power, social conflict, and democratic achievement in American society.

The development of union structure

As in Britain, trade unionism in America had its origins among the skilled craftsmen. Skilled workers had a vocational interest to protect, as well as the social skills necessary to form an organisation to increase their bargaining strength by combined action. The early unions were inevitably local organisations; their scope and scale were determined by the facts of geography, difficulties of communication, differences in habit and custom, and market conditions. These factors long deterred the development of national organisations, but as communications improved, the size of markets expanded, and the units of business operation grew, the unions were impelled by the same technological and social factors to mirror this growth in the pattern of their organisation. The tradition of local organisation – of local bargaining – had, however, taken deep root, and the structure of the national unions was shaped by this experience. In spite of the tremendous growth in the size of industrial establishments with the advent of mass-production processes, the craft unions were reluctant to make any fundamental change in the structure of their organisations that would admit the entry of the new class of machine tenders and general labourers who possessed no apprentice-trained skills.

The rigid adherence to principles which had served the craftsmen well, but which, without modification, failed to meet the needs of the mass-production workers, produced a violent explosion. Industrial unionism was born out of a bitter and unnecessary conflict that could have been averted by less selfishness and a greater willingness to compromise. In the event, the splitting of the American labour movement into two parts probably had a beneficial effect, since it compelled both sections to do their utmost to prove the validity of their actions. It was a case of competition proving to be the effective means of galvanising union leaders into a surge of activity that might never have been achieved had the movement remained united.

It is interesting to compare the path of union evolution in Britain with that in America. Before the First World War, when the theory of industrial unionism was first postulated, it was widely held that the disappearance of occupational-centred unions was inevitable with the growth of trusts and combines and the emergence of mass-production methods of manufacture. These developments were expected to result in a concentration of power that could only be matched by an all-embracing union. Since the new methods of production were eliminating skill, it was believed that craftsmen would disappear, to be replaced by unskilled operatives, who must be organised upon an industrial basis.

The theorists of industrial unionism were right in their opinion that the unskilled could not be organised, if selective entry qualifications were established and high entry fees and dues were charged; but they were quite wrong in their assumption that skilled work would become less important and skilled workers' unions would disappear. In fact, it is now apparent that the very opposite is taking place. It is the unskilled worker who is becoming redundant and being replaced in the modern mass-production factory by mechanical handling and electronic control devices.

British trade unions passed many resolutions in favour of industrial unionism, but the movement was never rent in twain by conflict, for two reasons. One was the simple fact that the unskilled were already being organised into their own organisations, and that this had been going on for twenty years before the birth of the industrial union movement. The second reason was the temper of the British trade unionist, who preferred to compromise and adjust rather than to make an issue of principle out of a question which was a matter of practical expediency. In any event, the outstanding features of the organisational development of British trade unionism in the twentieth century have been:

(1) the growth of the labourers' unions into great general unions which do not restrict their membership either by occupation or industry;

H

    (2) the evolution of the craft unions by opening up their membership to the semi-skilled and unskilled workers;

    (3) the growth of the non-manual workers' unions of clerks, civil servants, teachers, commercial employees, technicians, and professional, supervisory, and managerial staffs;

    (4) the welding of this complex of interweaving and overlapping groups into industrial federations for the purpose of collective bargaining.

Thus the structure of British trade unionism has not evolved according to a set pattern determined by a single theory of trade union organisation.

It is worthy of note that in the one industry in Britain where an industrial union was established as a deliberate exercise in the theory of scientific union organisation, there has been the most bitter history of inter-union conflict. The National Union of Railwaymen was the crowning achievement of the industrial union movement, and it was to be the 'New Model' that was to be followed in every other industry. However, in spite of an aggressive and persistent effort for more than forty years, the National Union of Railwaymen has failed to persuade the union which organises the railway clerical and supervisory staffs, and the union to which the locomotive engineers and firemen belong, to join forces in one big, all-grades industrial union. Even the N.U.R. itself, in spite of a continued emphasis on the significance of the industrial as distinct from the 'grade' concept of organisation, has had to meet rising pressure from its membership for more sectional representation.

Although British unions have shown much reluctance to amalgamate into industrial unions, they have had to evolve beyond the exclusive concepts and rigid notions of jurisdiction still held by some American craft unions. The growth of large-scale industry and the emergence of industry-wide collective bargaining has compelled unions that wished to retain occupation as a basic principle of organisation to find alternative methods of organisation that would permit the solution of problems that craft unionism had failed to resolve. British unions discovered that the device of federation would enable them to enjoy industry-wide bargaining whilst maintaining the community of interest which they find in belonging to occupationally based organisations.

The incentive to establish federal unions was provided by the growth of business combines, cartels, and trusts for the purpose of eliminating competition in the product market. At a later stage the employers founded associations for the purpose of collective bargaining. Thus, institutional arrangements were brought into being which made possible industry-wide bargaining without destroying established forms of trade union organisation.

At the stage when industrial unionism was being widely canvassed as the logically inevitable outcome of union growth and development, federations were looked upon as a halfway house, and were welcomed as stepping stones to this final goal. In fact, however, federations, joint industrial councils, wages boards, and other arrangements of similar kind have made industrial unionism unnecessary in so far as they have provided a solution to the problem of industry-wide bargaining without compelling the abandonment of union organisation based upon craft and occupational differences.

If federalism in one form or another is the principal device developed by British unions to preserve their institutional autonomy, the general union which spreads its area of recruitment across the boundaries of occupation and industry alike has been the most spectacular development in the growth of union organisation in the twentieth century.

General unions would appear to violate both the occupational and the industrial principle of organisation. It will be seen on closer examination, however, that, like federations, they provide a solution to the problem of more efficient organisation without destroying the basic desire for the separate representation of different occupational and industrial groups. Each of the large British general unions has satisfied, to a greater or lesser degree, within its constitutional framework, the conflicting demands of administration. In other words, general unions have succeeded because they have provided an institutional answer to the factors which have led to the breakdown of pure and simple craft unionism and of pure and simple industrial unionism.

The probability that American unions will combine to form large general unions on the British pattern at present appears small. There has been some tendency for this to happen in certain instances, but the experience of John L. Lewis's 'District Fifty' does not provide an exciting example for others to follow.* However, it is likely that the Teamsters' Union will prove to be an exception to the rule. This union has already succeeded in organising workers in a wide variety of trades and industries. It has the resources, and it might eventually find both the leadership and the dynamic to grow strongly in all directions, including that of white-collar workers. If it continues to expand its membership at the pace achieved in recent years, it will probably soon be very much larger than any of the industrial unions, which, unless they can find other ways of developing, will gradually contract as numbers employed in the mass-production industries are steadily reduced by the process of automation.

A development of this kind could be a major tragedy from the point of view of the role of American unions in society, since it is from the industrial unions, particularly the United Automobile Workers, that almost all the major developments in collective bargaining in the past twenty years have come. It is also impossible to avoid noticing that it is the industrial unions that have provided clean government and the closest ties with community activities. It is the Teamsters' and the craft unions that have clung to restrictive, out-of-date economic polices, that have shunned support for enlightened social developments, that have been the most easily penetrated by gangsters, and that have most strongly resisted attempts to enforce standards of honesty which would entail the ejection of the criminal elements who have frequently been elected to positions of power.

Whatever happens to the Teamsters', if industry-wide bargaining becomes a normal feature of American wage-fixing arrangements – and this may happen, as we shall show later – it is certain to affect trade union structure. Under such circumstances, unions will have to find a solution to opposing pressures; they will have to accommodate those making for further centralisation of control and those generated by the desire for sectional representation. It is possible that some kind of industrial federation could meet these new needs. A development of this kind would be even more in the general tradition of the American labour movement than the development that has taken place in Britain. There are examples of unions co-operating in multi-employer bargaining units, and there are clear

---

* This section of the Mineworkers' Union was prepared to recruit in any industry where it could gain members.

signs of federal arrangements being made by craft unions affiliated with the AFL-CIO Metal Trades Department for the purpose of collective bargaining. Unfortunately, this latter development has been inspired by hostility to the industrial unions, and it has generated fear that the craft organisations are bent on strengthening their position at the expense of the established industrial organisations. Inter-union conflict is far from being merely the product of dispute over rival forms of organisation; it often encompasses deep ideological differences and bitter personal jealousies and hatreds that are not easily overcome by rational argument.

Inter-union relations

Inter-union rivalry has proved to be a serious problem in most trade union movements throughout the world in which the principal basis of organisation was originally craft and occupation, but in no other country has conflict been so bitter and ruthless as in America.

In Europe, the problem of jurisdictional struggles was largely settled by the unions either adopting industrial unionism outright, as in Germany, or, as in Britain, by a willingness on the part of rival organisations to compromise their claims. Craft unions everywhere have put up a stout resistance to the encroachment of industrial unions, but under European conditions it has been possible to agree on a *modus vivendi* that has virtually eliminated the kind of deliberate assaults by one union upon another that take place in the United States.

In spite of the untidy trade union structure that exists in Britain, jurisdictional struggles have never loomed so large here as in the United States. Today, most unions in Britain have, in practice, a reasonably settled area of jurisdiction which is generally respected. Many unions have agreements with rival organisations establishing methods of resolving conflicts should they occur. The Trades Union Congress, which has played a cautious but important role in the conciliation of inter-union strife, has a well-developed procedure for investigating and settling jurisdictional disputes.

The Disputes Committee of the T.U.C. is empowered to summon the unions in conflict, hear evidence, and issue an award. The findings of the Committee must be carried out by the parties to the dispute; if they are not carried out the General Council has authority to suspend the offending organisation and to recommend to the annual meeting of the Trades Union Congress that it should be expelled. In the past thirty years the Disputes Committee has handled several hundred inter-union conflicts, but only in two cases has the Congress taken the drastic step of suspending and expelling; in each case the union involved was small and weak. The reluctance of the T.U.C. to expel a large organisation has been clearly seen in the rather special case of the E.T.U.; it finally took the plunge only after fraud was established in the Courts.

The less violent behaviour of British unions towards each other reflects basic differences in the two societies. Because Britain is older and smaller and has a more homogeneous, settled population, social relations are less sharp and compromise and tolerance are more easily achieved. The class structure of our society has tended to restrict competition, to make status more important than contract and convention more important than law. The institutions in the two countries often look alike and the principles applied are generally the same, but against the difference in background the outcome of their application is inevitably not always alike. The trend of social relations in America is towards a less competitive, more co-operative, and more harmonious way of life, but the 'rat race' is not over. The urge to get ahead, the fear of monopoly, the uninhibited egalitarianism of the dollar are powerful factors shaping American life. By comparison with Britain the pace in America is faster and the runners are more likely to turn round and rend their fellow competitors. But it is clear that unions and businessmen find the dynamic features of American society uncomfortable and they are constantly seeking to limit competition. If it were not for long-standing anti-trust legislation this trend would have gone much further.

Jurisdictional disputes were among the most important factors responsible for bringing the American Federation of Labour into being. However, the prevention of internecine struggle between American unions proved beyond the powers of the central body for many years. The biggest failure came when, rather than compromise, the craft unions accepted a fission in their ranks. This could have wrecked the organised labour movement for a long time, but in spite of the fact that organisational campaigns were marred by inter-union raiding, it proved to be a boon, since it stimulated a vigorous drive to secure members at a time when there was plenty of scope for union growth.

The more responsible union leaders in both the AFL and the CIO eventually came to see little virtue in stealing members from one another, like rustlers in the days of the wild west. When they eventually decided to merge into one organisation, the abolition of raiding was one of the most important points in the minds of the AFL-CIO leaders.

The adoption of the no-raiding pact was a landmark in the history of the American labour movement, and one that may well prove to be fraught with many consequences. The pact has inevitably compelled affiliated unions to pay more respect to the central organisation. Like the British T.U.C., upon which it was modelled, the AFL has always sought to avoid interference in the domestic affairs of its affiliated organisations. The principle of autonomous government, which was regarded as sacrosanct by the craft unions in the AFL, was never accepted to quite the same degree by the CIO. This was for the very good reason that the most important unions in the CIO – automobile, steel, and electrical – owed their existence to the efforts of the central body. These unions did not already have a long tradition of independent membership before they came into the central organisation. Thus, the merger with the CIO strengthened the tendency, already in evidence, for the AFL to move away from its original position.

Growth in the power of the AFL-CIO

Many other factors have contributed to the increase in the prestige and authority of the central body. Perhaps the most important of these over the long run has been the extension of government interference in and control over the social and economic life of the nation. Two wars and the needs of defence have changed the dimension of governmental responsibilities. Except for an extreme minority, it is now accepted by all sections of the community that the government, federal and state, has a major responsibility for keeping the economic affairs of the nation on an even keel. This includes social welfare and the development and conservation of the human and physical resources of the nation.

As the public welfare under modern conditions has come increasingly to depend upon the activities of the federal and state authorities, the significance of the central trade union organisation has grown *pari passu*. For effective action on problems that were of concern to all sections of their membership and the community at large, the unions had to have a spokesman for their common interests. Both the AFL and the CIO gained enormously in prestige and status during the war, and in the post-war decade their public position has grown ever more important. The merger between the two organisations and its successful consolidation has further advanced this standing.

It would be true to say of trade unionism in America what Sir Winston Churchill once said of the British trade union movement, that it has become an 'estate of the realm'. By this description, Sir Winston meant that as a social institution to which millions gave their loyalty, the trade union movement rightly enjoyed great influence and prestige, and that the public had a right to expect in return that it would exercise its power with a sense of responsibility to the community as well as to its own members.

Thus the efforts of the AFL-CIO to check inter-union fights, which have been crowned with considerable success, and the ethical practices codes, which have already proved to be of profound importance and are bringing a new and closer relationship between the central body and its constituent associations, must be set in the context of social and economic trends that make such developments inevitable. Neither in Britain nor in the United States have the activities and authority of the central bodies been extended so far as their opposite numbers in Holland, the Scandinavian countries, and Germany. There are, however, factors in the current industrial and social environment which point to the AFL-CIO acquiring more responsibilities and authority to speak and act on behalf of the unions as a whole. The recent recession has emphasised the importance of federal economic and social policy. The election of Senator Kennedy and the return of the Democrats to power has provided new opportunities for the leaders of the AFL-CIO to press for developments that they believe will benefit the unions and their members. It is conceivable, but extremely unlikely, that the struggle with the Teamsters' Union, expelled on grounds of corrupt leadership,*

* See the following: Interim Report of the Select Committee on Improper Activities in the Labor or Management Field, U.S. Senate Report No. 1417, 85th Congress, March 1958; hearings before the Sub-Committee on Labor of the Committee on Labor and Public Welfare, U.S. Senate, 85th Congress, Second Session on Union Financial and Administrative Practices and Procedures, March 1958; Professor John Hutchinson, 'Corruption in American Trade Unions', *Political Quarterly*, July-September, 1957.

might destroy the power and prestige of the AFL-CIO, but if that were to happen, dissident unions would probably soon form a new central organisation or return to the rump of the old one and give it new life and new leaders. The Teamsters' Union is itself an example of the powerful forces that, under modern conditions, unless deliberately checked, make for the centralisation of government and administration of social institutions.

Growth in union size

The typical trade union today is a large-scale organisation; in every industrial country the size of the unions has been steadily increasing. Big unionism is a product of the same complex of factors that has produced big business. Bigness is invariably looked upon by businessmen and union leaders as an index of their success. It is justified on grounds of maximising efficiency by both business men and trade unionists. In the case of the union, size is equated with bargaining strength, increased union security, and lower operating costs.

This view of the advantages of large-scale organisation is not always borne out by the facts. The fates of the Grand National Consolidated trade union in England and the Knights of Labour in America are historical reminders that size alone is not enough to guarantee viability. The strength of a union rests on many factors of which size is only one. Small unions in trades where they can exercise a decisive role over the supply of labour, and enjoy the unstinted loyalty and support of their members, are often in a much stronger bargaining position than many a giant. It is this factor that provides a powerful incentive to craft unions to preserve their identity in face of demands for amalgamation with massive industrial unions.

The principal advantage of large-scale unionism lies in the ability to provide a range of services which a small union would find too costly. Unfortunately, the advantages of bigness have to be set against the adverse effects which large-scale units have on the practice of democracy. The degree to which members participate in union activities and the extent to which leaders are able to dominate the rank and file is closely correlated with the size of the units of organisation.

As unions get larger, leaders inevitably become more remote and more difficult to control. The size of the unit of government is particularly important at the local level. In order to maintain the maximum degree of rank and file participation, many British unions fix a maximum size for their local units of organisation. When units are small, it is possible for rank-and-file officers to run them with the minimum of assistance from a professional union representative attached to the district or regional level. But when the size of a local reaches a certain point, it becomes necessary to employ a full-time business agent, whose principal function is to service the local's contracts. This practice is widespread in the United States.

The nature of collective bargaining in the United States, with its separate plant contracts, highly detailed contents, and well-developed grievance machinery, including arbitration, necessarily calls for professional assistance. Under the British system, in which agreements are generally confined to a very limited range of items, and where there is no elaborate system of grievance arbitration based on the detailed clauses of a legally binding contract, there is much less requirement for professional assistance at the local level. It is the exception rather than the rule to find the local unit of trade union organisation in charge of a full-time, paid agent.

Although large locals often develop bureaucratic characteristics, the fact that they are big and strong permits them to stand up to domination from the international centre. Thus we find the paradox that small units of organisation, which permit the maximum degree of membership participation, also permit a high degree of central control. Large locals, which are generally less democratically governed, frequently prevent power from being overwhelmingly concentrated in the hands of the international president.

When dealing with the problems generated by 'bigness' it is important not to fall into the trap of romanticising the advantages of 'smallness'. What is significant in union organisation as in business is not size *per se,* but the appropriate scale for the function. It is necessary in certain instances that a decision be taken on the widest possible scale; in others there is no reason why uniformity should extend beyond the smallest group. What is required is to adjust union structures so as to take into account these various needs and to balance administrative convenience and efficiency against the promotion of membership participation and democratic control. It is one of the ironies of the American situation that the device of chartering locals, which was designed to permit locals the maximum degree of autonomy, may well have the effect of making union structures more rigid and more undemocratic than would be the case if it were possible to revise them on the basis of a careful investigation of the problems and objectives they were devised to achieve.

It must be admitted that local autonomy has permitted unsavoury people to reach positions of power in many American unions. From this situation there has developed the need to put locals under the control of the International, in order to oust the discredited leadership. Since new leaders are not always easy to find, or would not necessarily be strong enough to overcome the powers of resistance displayed by the expelled faction, it is frequently necessary to maintain the local under the trusteeship of the International for a long time. This procedure may, however, be used for the unlawful purpose of ejecting *bona fide* local leaders in order to maintain in power a corrupt international leadership. This problem is the subject of the AFL-CIO ethical codes and it is covered by the Labour Management Reporting and Disclosure Act, but these measures are not in themselves likely to provide the answer to the question of creating the most appropriate union structure for modern conditions. This can only be found by union leaders and members who are determined to maintain a democratic organisation, to resist the pressures leading to the centralisation of power and who are prepared to fight continuously against the abuse of their rights and obligations.

III

Union Democracy

THE American pattern of political democracy often turns out to be a conflict for power in which only the roughest edges of the struggle are smoothed by the rules that have been developed over the centuries. However much the outsider might feel that every candidate, every vested interest, doth protest too much, he cannot but marvel at the recurring vitality, at the constant surge of snarling, snapping intolerant criticism of the politicians who for the time being fiercely cling to office. Even in those areas where only one party is ever elected, there is no degeneration into easy-going complacency. Opposition wells up like oil in Texas, within and without the party, and those who are 'in' have to maintain a constant vigilance to prevent themselves from being pushed out by the burgeoning of aspirants for office. Whatever criticisms could be launched against the American political system, it certainly could not be said that it had been overtaken by the 'iron law of oligarchy'; opposition is omnipresent.

When we turn to the trade union field we find that opposition to the established leadership is often feeble and quite often non-existent. The situation which appears now to prevail in many of the most important trade unions contrasts vividly with the robust character of democracy at the national and state level of government; it has been likened to that of the one-party state.* The terminology is, perhaps, misleading, but it would appear that there is only one American union which bears any resemblance to the national system of democracy, and that is the International Typographical Union. This union has a two-party system of government;

* S. M. Lipset, M. A. Trow, J. S. Coleman, *Union Democracy*, The Free Press, Glencoe, Ill., 1956.

124

there is a recognised opposition which is at all times ready to provide an alternative leadership, policy, and programme, to that of the incumbents.

Most unions, in most countries, are not based upon a party system. The rule followed by unions all over the world is, with few exceptions, what might best be described as individual democracy. That is to say, members have a right in their individual capacity to elect their leaders and to decide issues of policy by majority rule, but not to combine in any organised group to exercise these functions. Many unions in America, Britain, and elsewhere have rules specifically designed to prevent their members from forming factions or parties. The fear behind these rules is that the formation of organised groups may result in conflicts that would tear the unions apart. This danger is obviously present, but the prohibition of all forms of organised opposition may well present an even greater danger: that of entrenching a leadership that is unpopular, inefficient, and even corrupt.

In some unions the rights of members have been flagrantly violated by union leaders intent on keeping power at all costs. In others, the authority, prestige, and monopoly of the union's media of communication is combined to make any successful challenge to the established position of the leaders a remote possibility. The more flagrant examples of methods used to ensure the defeat of an opposition, such as by the chartering of 'phoney locals', the disqualification of ballots from hostile locals, the elimination of criticism by imposing trusteeship, have only been used in a minority of instances.* Less crude, but equally effective and equally undemocratic, is the crushing of opposition by accusations of attempting to foment rival unionism, discrediting its leadership by false accusations of collusion with employers, communists, and other union foes.

There are of course unions with leaderships that are models of probity, efficiency, and responsibility, but even the most enlightened look upon opposition with a jaundiced eye and give it no encouragement. Supported by the power of a well-organised machine, the position of the top leaders in unions almost everywhere is well-nigh unassailable. American union leaders appear, however, to have

---

* The election of James Hoffa was allegedly secured by votes from locals which only existed on paper and by disqualifying on technical grounds votes from locals known to be against Hoffa.

achieved a position of supremacy that goes far beyond what is normal in many other countries. In terms of security of tenure there is, perhaps, little to choose between union leaders in Europe or the United States. However, it is worth pointing out that almost all the major unions in Britain have a retiring age of 65 for their paid officers, and in one or two unions it is even as low as 60 years.

The official attitude of union leaders in America as, for example, recently expressed by 75-year-old Luigi Antonini, a vice-president of the International Ladies' Garment Workers' Union, is that they die in harness. Once elected, union leaders are determined to stay in office until senile decay or death compels retirement. Defeat is not accepted as a risk inherent in the job, as it is by any democratic politician. Not only do incumbents refuse to accept the possibility of personal defeat, but the accession to office of their chosen successor has now become a matter of prestige. Thus, even the succession is often removed from the choice of the members.

It is far more common in European countries for union leaders to be elected only after a genuine contest which involves the choice of the rank-and-file union members than it is in America. It is of course true that the successful contestant can often be predicted because of the opportunities provided by his previous position to win popular support; nevertheless the rank-and-file membership are able to exercise the right to vote between rival candidates. It is quite certain that no man reaches the top position in an American union without overcoming considerable opposition; a power struggle within the confines of a machine is not, however, a substitute for an election which involves the effective participation of the rank-and-file. Democratic rights may die from atrophy equally as effectively as from crude violations of the essential constitutional requirements of democracy.

Once elected, the power of an American union president generally far exceeds that of any officer of British or Scandinavian unions. The authority enjoyed by the president of an American union stems from a concept of government derived from that of the United States. It is that the president should be the supreme executive, with authority to determine policy, and to appoint staff and paid officials of the organisation. Unfortunately, the checks and balances adopted by trade unions do not compare with those which restrain the activities of a President of the United States.

The provision in a union's constitution for regular election of officers may mean little, if by default or design no contest takes place. In the nation state, it is the existence of political parties which ensures that electors will have a choice of candidates. In a union there is often no such mechanism, since the collective organisation of opposition is frowned upon and any manifestation of it is with rare exceptions vigorously squashed. Therefore, if elections are to be regularly contested, union members must be allowed to campaign for their nominee and to have access to the media of communication, so as to disseminate their ideas on policy and programme. This is not a matter of fundamental change in union constitutions, but it requires a willingness on the part of union leaders to accept democracy as a desirable method of union government.

At present, union leaders declare their faith in democracy, but in practice this frequently turns out to be no more than lip service to the idea. Democracy is certainly an uncomfortable doctrine to live with, but it is only by the establishment of rival centres of power and deep respect for its rules and conventions that it is kept alive in the state. For democracy to be made real in a union, and for that matter in any other large-scale organisation, a similar situation must prevail.

What is not permissible, since it violates the spirit of democracy, if not always the rules, is that there should be any clandestine organisation. In this respect, the methods of the Communists are well known. They have frequently captured power in both American and European unions for two reasons.* One is the apathy of the non-Communist majorities; the second, the rules and conventions against factions. Taking advantage of light polls, of the reluctance of non-Communists to violate the rules relating to collective action, and of the traditional dislike of witch-hunting or of interference with established rights, Communists have had a clear run to capture power. They have not scrupled to ignore the rules and, by secret organisation, to pack meetings, organise support for their candidate, and, where they hold office, to engage in fraud to ensure that he is elected.

In Europe, as well as in America, these tactics have stimulated efforts to defeat the Communists at their own game. It has been

* David J. Saposs, *Communism in American Unions*, McGraw-Hill, 1959.

shown overwhelmingly that the most powerful weapon against the Communists is complete exposure of the party character of their activities. In other words, it is necessary to abandon the notion of individual democracy and to permit factions to fight factions. In fact, this situation often exists in British unions and, to a very large extent, elections are conducted on political lines, with Communists and left-wing elements forming a constant source of opposition. Thus, union elections are kept alive, and members are presented with a choice of candidates, in spite of rules which attempt to suppress factionalism.

It is of vital importance that members be aware of the existence of rival candidates, and that those who are standing for office have the right to put their point of view either in the union journal or in other ways. It is completely undemocratic of incumbent union leaders to deny rival candidates any access to the members during an election campaign. There may be a case for not allowing critics of the leaders an unlimited access to the columns of the union's journal, but they ought to be given some opportunity to state their views, if only in the letters-to-the-editor column. At election times they should be entitled to issue an election address. It would be reasonable to insist upon the material conforming to certain standards. Personal abuse of rival candidates might properly be outlawed, and a maximum length, period of issue, and so forth, set for the mutual benefit of all. Another reasonable step is to print an agreed short biography of each candidate on the ballot, so that the voter has at least the minimum information required to make a fair choice.

There is much to be said in favour of making certain essential electoral procedures legally enforceable, as provided for in the Labour Management Reporting and Disclosure Act. It was a step in the right direction to compel a union to inform every member of the time and place of elections, if they differ from the time laid down in the union's rules, to give each member in good standing opportunity to nominate candidates, and to vote without coercion or restraint. The rights of members will also be advanced now that incumbent officers are prevented from using union funds to promote their own re-election.

Such measures as these, in themselves, may fall short of what is required to stimulate the re-birth of democratic union elections. For their effectiveness, much will depend upon their observance and enforcement by officers and members. However, in this respect an important innovation, which could prove to be of outstanding significance, has been introduced by the Labour Management Reporting and Disclosure Act. It provides that any member of a labour organisation who, having exhausted the remedies available under its constitution and by-laws, feels that his rights have not been respected, may file a complaint with the Secretary of Labour. The Secretary of Labour is now empowered by law to investigate the allegations and, if he finds cause to believe that a violation of the Act has occurred and has not been remedied, to bring a civil action against the union in an appropriate District Court. There he would seek to have the election set aside as invalid, and to obtain the authority of the Court to conduct a fresh election under the supervision of the Secretary, under such rules and regulations as the Secretary might prescribe.

Thus the member can be provided with the powerful support of a public agency which bears the brunt of the expense, worry, and effort that is required to secure a remedy against injustice and the violation of democratic rights. The success of this idea will, of course, depend upon the initiative and political integrity of the members and the Secretary of Labour, and the willingness of the Courts to act vigorously and promptly. There are good grounds for hoping that these qualities will not be lacking. A rather similar procedure has proved effective in important circumstances in Australia.

Even if the right to choose their leaders is effectively restored to the rank and file of unions, this, in itself, will not be enough to ensure that unions are led in a democratic fashion. The forces making for the centralisation of decision-making and administration are too strong to be resisted except by deliberate action. Contested union elections must be supported by several other changes.

Control of the executive

The power of union presidents to make decisions in the name of the union should be drastically curtailed. The situation in which a union president finds himself is not analogous to that of the chief executive in the state. Union presidents do not have to submit their programmes to a congress which may change the proposals submitted. The union convention, unfortunately, appears to have become, in many cases, little more than an organised claque. Issues

I

are often not debated on the floor of the convention. Open opposition is frowned upon and disagreements are ironed out in smoke-filled hotel rooms. Fights between leaders jockeying to obtain the top position may indicate that the incumbent president is not an absolute monarch, but the pattern is more akin to the way in which policy is made and changes in the leadership are determined in the Soviet Union than in the United States. Bossism is recognised as an ugly feature of American politics and, as a result of a hostile public reaction, it is now much reduced in scale. It has, however, to be dealt with in the unions and perhaps, ultimately, it may be dealt with in business enterprise, where it also exists.*

It would be a healthy development if the senior officers of unions were subject to the control of an executive committee of the rank and file. The dangers to democracy which occur when the chief executive officers are directly elected by the rank and file and do not face the check of an elected lay committee was stressed by the Webbs more than sixty years ago, when they published the results of their famous inquiries into British unions. It is worthy of note, in this respect, that the American Bakery and Confectionery Workers' Union, which was created after its predecessor had been expelled from the AFL-CIO because of its corrupt leadership, has adopted a constitution which provides that ten of its eighteen executive board members must be elected from the union's five regions and may not be on the payroll of the International. This arrangement may be contrasted with the situation in the expelled union, where a majority of the executive board were on the International staff, and therefore responsible to the president for their appointment. A further new development is the establishment of a special panel of twenty local union officers, none of whom may be paid officers of the International, with sole authority to put a local into trusteeship. No trusteeship may last longer than six months without a hearing by this panel.

It is, of course, always possible that a lay executive committee becomes merely the agent of a determined president. If, however, the executive must be re-elected at regular intervals, and the tradition of contested elections is developed, it is far less likely that an

* Cf. William M. Lieserson, *American Trade Union Democracy*, Columbia University Press, 1959; Philip Taft, *The Structure and Government of Labour Unions*, Harvard University Press, 1954.

executive of rank-and-file members will be as pliant as an executive board of paid vice-presidents, each of whom owes his position to support of the senior officer.

If democracy in the unions is to be preserved, it is of the utmost importance that responsibility and authority be diffused. This means that the pattern of collective bargaining ought to be kept as local as possible. The bargaining unit is frequently determined by factors that are beyond the control of the union, and the trends are clearly in the direction of more centralised bargaining. In these circumstances, it is essential that vigorous steps be taken to keep the rank and file informed and to permit them to share in the process of policy making. Some unions already pay attention to this factor and give their members a responsible role.

Locals have often been allowed to grow into units that are far too large and cover much too wide an area for the successful preservation of democracy. The ideal unit of organisation is a local based upon a plant or other homogeneous unit of production. This is certainly not always possible, and the structure of locals must necessarily take into account the pattern of industrial organisation. In the past, union structure has been determined primarily by factors of power, and empire-building propensities. Now it is time that careful consideration be given to the needs of democracy.

It is also important that national union leaders do not abuse their ultimate authority over union locals by the imposition of trusteeship or other devices designed to deprive local union members of their rights. There is clearly a legitimate use of trusteeship and supervision of a local by the International – it may well be necessary, and in the interest of democracy. It is proper, however, that this power should be controlled, and proposals that have been embodied in the Labour Management Reporting and Disclosure Act do not seem unreasonable in the light of the evidence presented to the Senate Committee on Improper Activities in the Labour or Management Field. Under this Act, every labour organisation which assumes a trusteeship over any subordinate body is compelled to file a report which, *inter alia,* must include a detailed statement of the reason for establishing the trusteeship, and the nature and extent to which members of the local are to be allowed to participate in the selection of delegates to represent them at union conventions and in the election of officers. The Secretary of Labour is charged with the responsibility of investigating allegations that the trusteeship has not been imposed in accordance with the constitution, and for the purpose of correcting malpractices or the violation of collective bargaining agreements. If the Secretary finds that *prima facie* there is a case to be answered, he is enjoined to bring a civil action, without disclosing the identity of the complainant, to secure such relief from the violation as may be appropriate. Since it is now widely agreed that no trusteeship should be continued indefinitely without steps being taken to ensure that there are good grounds for its extension, it is also appropriate that the law should make certain that this safeguard is provided.

These proposals when first made aroused a certain amount of criticism, but if members cannot rely upon their International Union, under all circumstances, to see that their rights are not abused, it is necessary to invoke the aid of public agencies. The idea of making the Secretary of Labour an active guardian of the rights of union members, but only to the extent of initiating action in the Courts, may prove highly salutary, so long as the task is carried out with purpose and discretion.

Appeals procedure

Every union must be able to exercise certain powers of discipline over members who carelessly, or intentionally, violate the rules. In cases where members deliberately refuse to accept decisions constitutionally arrived at, and behave in such a way as to threaten the stability of the organisation, it is perfectly legitimate that they should be expelled. The power of expulsion is a drastic weapon, and it should only be used when it can be clearly proved that the member concerned has wilfully broken the rules to which he subscribed when joining the organisation. It is essential that a man should not be expelled on vague and dubious charges of promoting 'dual unionism' merely because he has exercised the right of criticising the incumbent leaders and of seeking to promote opposition to them. In order to safeguard the interests of the members in this respect, the rules of a union ought to make provision for a trial and appeals procedure which satisfies the rules of 'natural justice', or, as it would be put in America, 'due process'. No member should be expelled without having received a clear notice of the charge, which should be specifically defined in the rules of the union. He should be given adequate time to prepare his defence and served with a proper notice of the time and date of the trial, which should be held in an area adjacent to his place of work or residence. He should be allowed to be represented by a person of his own choice, to state his case fully, and to examine evidence and witnesses against him. Above all, he should be allowed to appeal to a body which has no vested interest in the outcome of the case. It is entirely contrary to the rules of natural justice that a union executive board should act in a capacity where, like old Fury, it is involved as both judge and jury in its own cause. Some unions elect entirely separate appeals courts from the rank-and-file membership. An even better idea is the outside review board consisting of prominent disinterested citizens, such as has been established by the Upholsterers' Union and the Automobile Workers. A body of this kind inspires far greater confidence than any union committee could, and a member who has been made the subject of serious disciplinary action has no grounds for complaint that his appeal has not been fairly decided.

If the rights to which a member is entitled by a union constitution are violated, he is at liberty to bring a suit against the offending party in the Courts. This is an essential feature of the rule of law and a basic protection against the breach of contractual rights by a stronger party. In protecting the union member from arbitrary and unjust acts of union officials, the British courts have, in recent years, made a significant contribution to the preservation of union democracy. They have, in a series of notable cases, demonstrated that union members must be treated strictly in accordance with the union constitution. Any violation of the rights of the member may entail an award of damages for breach of contract. What is perhaps of even greater significance in the long run is the *obiter dictum* of Lord Justice Denning, that the Courts would look upon any rule which purported to exclude the Courts from examining and interpreting union rules as contrary to public policy and, therefore, null and void.

Self-regulation

Reliance on the law is, however, an inadequate substitute for self-regulation. The Courts have themselves recognised this, since they usually insist upon a union member exhausting the remedies provided under the constitution of his organisation before they will consider his complaint. There is much to be said for this attitude if it does not result in the denial of justice to a member whose rights have been violated. In this respect, the decision of the Committee on Ethical Practices of the AFL-CIO to draft a code of the basic and elementary principles which should be followed by every affiliated union is important, and an example the British T.U.C. might adopt with advantage.

The code states, *inter alia*:

1. That every member should have the right to equal treatment in the application of union rules and laws; that it is essential that the principles of due process should be observed; and that provision should be made for appeals to a higher body.

2. That each member has the responsibility to (*a*) fully exercise his rights; (*b*) loyally to support his union, but not to advocate dual unionism, to destroy, to weaken the union as a collective bargaining agency, or to carry on libel and slander.

3. To safeguard the rights of the member, each affiliated union should hold regular conventions at not more than four-year intervals.

4. Officers, and other officials given authority to govern, should be elected by referendum or by vote of the delegates to a convention.

5. All general conventions should be open to the public and a summary should be available to the members.

6. Membership meetings of local unions should take place at regular intervals at a time and place that has been given proper notice.

7. Union officers should not be elected to a term running longer than four years.

8. To ensure democratic, responsible, and honest administration, the AFL-CIO and affiliated unions should have the power to institute disciplinary and corrective proceedings and establish trusteeships where necessary.

9. Where constitutional amendments are required to conform to these standards the AFL-CIO expect that they will be made at the earliest moment.

This code is excellent in intention, but it is by no means an easy task, except in cases of outrageous violation, to compel unions to live up to it. If the affiliated unions could be persuaded to agree to the establishment of a review board of the type established by the UAW, to operate as a kind of union supreme court under the sponsorship of the AFL-CIO, this would greatly reinforce the steps taken by the central body to lay down minimum standards.

In the last resort, however, the problem of union democracy depends upon the willingness of union officers to respect the rights of the members that are embodied in a union constitution. The difference between the Teamsters' Union and the United Automobile Workers lies not so much in their constitutions as in the quality of their respective leaderships. In the one, leadership is in the hands of men whose behaviour, as shown by the evidence given to Senate Committees, proves they care little for moral standards. However, the fact that leaders of the Teamsters' have been shown to be venal individuals does not mean that they have not been successful in obtaining substantial improvements in conditions of employment, or that they will not do their utmost to protect their members if any of them get into trouble. This is not, of course, democracy; it is the paternalism of men satisfying their egos with the fruits of their dubious activities and deceiving themselves and their members that they are behaving honourably. If every rogue was let off because he had done a good turn with somebody else's money, the world would be full of people playing Robin Hood and no one's property would be safe from depredations.

The UAW is firmly governed and it is hardly conceivable that Reuther and his associates would readily permit themselves to be thrown out of office, but they would never seek to defeat their opponents by hiring thugs, by blackmail, or by wholesale bribery and corruption. They would use the techniques of democracy, the arts of writing and speech, and the process of education to underpin their position and ensure that they remained in command. It may be objected that this comes to the same thing; in both cases the leadership is strongly entrenched. Criticism of this kind does, however, miss the essential point. Strong government is not antithetical to democracy; it is the way that power is achieved and maintained that is of fundamental importance. In Reuther's case, it was achieved in accordance with standards that are accepted in every civilized state as constituting the essence of democracy; and every effort has been made to maintain these standards.

The right to choose a union

However perfect a union constitution might be, and however well-intentioned union officers might be, the danger that power might corrupt their performance is ever-present. It is therefore of some considerable importance that union members should be able to vote with their feet as well as with their hands. A decline in membership may well be a salutary reminder to a leadership that has abused its position that it cannot continue to violate the rights of members without incurring dangerous consequences. This check, under modern conditions, has unfortunately been rendered almost inoperative.

One reason why this check is not so important as it ought to be is simply that union members may be so apathetic, bullied, and browbeaten by union leaders, or fearful of facing their employer without union support, as to prefer to avoid even the semblance of a challenge to those in power. Another reason is that workers have, to no small extent, had their freedom to choose whether they will belong to a union, and to which one, considerably curtailed by the legal support given to unions since the passing of the National Labour Relations Act in 1935. The purpose behind the system of certifying an exclusive bargaining agent and in legally sanctioning the union shop was to protect the union against the union-wrecking activities of employers. It is true that under the Wagner and Taft-Hartley Acts union members are not prevented from joining another union, in spite of the fact that the one to which they belong has been granted an exclusive bargaining jurisdiction. But if there is a union shop contract, they cannot cease paying their contributions until the contract ends. The policy of the NLRB has, in fact, been to discourage switching, and it is no easy matter to defeat a union that has consolidated bargaining rights. The Taft-Hartley Act underlines the official opposition to inter-union conflict by making jurisdictional strikes over representation illegal. When these legal procedures are supplemented by AFL-CIO sponsored no-raiding pacts, designed to consolidate the present pattern of jurisdiction, the element of choice left to a worker is extremely small.

There is, of course, a strong case for the no-raiding agreement on grounds of public policy, since fights over membership and jurisdiction are at the expense of the innocent, and they also waste union resources and bring discredit to labour organisations. But when a corrupt union is able to obtain a decision in its favour from the Courts restraining a rival organisation from taking its members on the grounds of the no-raiding agreement, it is obvious that the solution of one problem has worsened another. It is, in fact, almost impossible for any group of workers to transfer their allegiance from one affiliated union to another without running foul of the no-raiding rules which the courts have decreed must be observed by the NLRB when ruling on demands for a certification election by a rival union.

Whatever might be said in favour of the legal support given to unionism during the past quarter of a century, there can be little doubt that from the point of view of promoting union democracy the emphasis which has been given to union security has had an unfortunate effect. It has encouraged autocratic leadership, consolidated an inevitable tendency towards bureaucracy, and cut off a source of the dynamic effort required to sustain democracy.

In view of the history of the American labour movement, the pathological concern of unions with the maintenance of their institutional security ought to be well understood. Trade unionism is a feature of every industrialised country in the world, but in no other country has the battle to obtain recognition, legal and social status, been so bloody and so bitter. In this respect, the history of American labour relations reflects the intolerance of a vital, expanding society, which for a long time ruthlessly swept aside attempts to curb the right of the owners of property to exploit the working-people as they saw fit.* The reluctance of the American conservative to compromise in his attitude to labour, to the extent of genuinely accepting unions as an inevitable and valuable feature of a modern industrial society, has had the tragic consequence of making the security of their organisation an almost fanatical obsession with the leaders of labour unions.

The irony of the situation was that the failure of employers to accept the unions led to the adoption of legislation which not only drastically curtailed their freedom to refuse to recognise that unions

* For an excellent account of the history of trade unions in the United States see F. R. Dulles, *Labour in America*.

existed, but consolidated the power of the leader 'outside' their enterprise. This, the very thing that they feared most, was stimulated and strengthened. In the event, many large American employers have now recognised that unionism cannot be dislodged by the tactics of Jay Gould or Henry Ford, and they have decided that collusion is more profitable than valorous opposition.

At the level of the big corporation, management has learnt to live with the unions, but some of America's leading companies spend large sums of money counter-attacking labour organisations. They feel this to be necessary, not because they have much hope of putting the unions out of business, but to keep them at bay.

At the level of the smaller firm, management is still often reluctant to recognise that unions are here to stay and persistently twists and turns, sometimes displaying a ferocious antagonism to escape their attentions.

This difference in the attitudes of business is to be explained in part by the vulnerability of the firms to competitive pressures, in part to the greater separation of ownership and managerial control at the level of the larger enterprise, and in part by the personal idiosyncrasies of leaders on both sides.

If democracy is to be stimulated rather than repressed in the unions, it will be necessary to make legal changes. In many respects it would be a good thing to repeal the Taft-Hartley Act entirely, so that unions and employers would have to find a mutual accommodation without the artificial aid of the law. Such an ideal solution is, however, no more than an idle dream; there is by now far too big a vested interest in the system for it to be abandoned. The problem is, then, a matter of reforming the law so as to stimulate democracy without undermining union security and stable industrial relations.

To many business men and others the obvious legal reform is the outlawing of compulsory unionism, by the adoption of right to work laws.

Unions describe the right to refuse to join a trade union as a 'phoney right'. They stigmatise workers who, on refusing to join a union, invoke the right of association as a fundamental liberty of the private citizen in a free society, as frauds who are merely bent upon obtaining the benefits of unionism without discharging their obligation to contribute at least their dues. That there are grounds for moral indignation cannot be denied, but the question that has to

be answered is whether the evil done by making union membership a condition of employment is larger or smaller than the effects
of legally protecting a person who wishes to contract out of the
association.

It is doubtful whether this problem can, in fact, be solved by
citing moral propositions and claiming them to be categorical
imperatives. The freedom of association principle is in direct conflict with the principle that no man is entitled to enjoy the fruits
of common effort if he is not himself prepared to contribute. The
problem can, therefore, only be resolved by reference to a wider
set of criteria. These might be examined in relation to the problems
firstly of union security, and secondly of the democratic rights of
individuals in relation to the union and society.

Union leaders fear that in the absence of legally sanctioned compulsion unions will not be able to maintain their membership without at least a vast increase in effort that will be extremely costly in
time and money. Paid union officials will have to spend a large
part of their day on the business of organising; merely to maintain
the membership in good standing will require much more activity
than is necessary when members are compelled to belong to the
union to hold their jobs and the employer has agreed to check off
their dues from their wages.

To the leaders of the unions, all this seems to be wasted effort,
and much less efficient than the simple method of reaching their
goal of one hundred per cent membership by making membership
a condition of employment. It is also pointed out that union officials
who have to spend a great deal of their time on maintaining membership have less time to spend on promoting union democracy
and giving good service to union members. In fact, it could be
argued that union officials may well be encouraged to use undemocratic pressures to achieve membership goals in the absence
of compulsory conditions. Above all, the right-to-work law is a
threat to the security of the union leader. It is an affront to his
dignity, since it puts him at the mercy of the unsophisticated rank-
and-file, for whose judgement on issues of collective bargaining
he has a professional distrust. Many union leaders of today deeply
resent the fact that they cannot look a business man in the face
without being aware that they have less security and, as a result,
less status in the *milieu* in which they move.

It must be admitted that compulsory unionism solves the fundamental problem of maintaining membership and ensuring a steady
flow of union dues. Clearly, this will not be regarded with favour
by those who see unions as evil institutions, but what they perhaps
do not realise is that a union might become a much more vigorous
and militant organisation if it does not have the security provided
by a 'union shop' agreement.

It is precisely on this point that many strong supporters of trade
unions as vital components in a pluralist society criticise compulsory unionism. They see in the very nature of the case made out
in its favour by union leaders the seeds of the decay of union
democracy, and with it the militancy which they consider essential
to the preservation of a healthy system of industrial relations.

From the point of view of the individual, the right-to-work law,
which safeguards his job, in so far as the union cannot demand
that he should be dismissed for non-payment of dues, places him
in a stronger position *vis-à-vis* the paid union officer than would
otherwise be the case. It does not follow, however, that workers
would be constantly exercising the right to quit the union, or that
they would look with moral approval on those who did not pay
union dues.

The overwhelming support for 'union shop' contracts in the period
when ballots on this issue were compulsory, provides some indica-
tion of current feelings. This is supported by the long history of
support in unions and professional organisations for compulsory
membership. Here, then, is the problem. Most workers in America
are in favour of compulsory unionism, but there is usually a
minority in every factory, mine or mill who would prefer to stay
out. There is only one way in which to satisfy the conflict of this
typically human desire, and that is by the abandonment of abso-
lutist positions. This means that the demand of the union for
security is proper in a society which accepts trade unionism as a
socially desirable activity, but only in so far as it is 'reasonable'
and not absolute security. Reasonable security is not, however, the
same as compelling every worker to become a member as a condition of employment. It is enough from this point of view that the
majority of workers in a particular unit of employment should
belong.

The unions' fear that the abandonment of compulsory membership would inevitably lead to dire consequences ought to be put to a proper test. If it proved to have any serious validity, then it would be necessary to reconsider the situation. It would very probably turn out that the unions were as wrong in their analysis of the effect of right-to-work laws as they were in their predictions about the consequences of the Taft-Hartley Act. If this probability turned out to be correct, then the employers, who are ardent advocates of right-to-work laws for the wrong reasons, would be disappointed.

Sooner or later those American employers who feel that somehow unions must be crippled will have to realise that trade unions are the product of powerful social forces and that they cannot be swept away, in a free society, by law, by ruthless opposition, or by the exercise of deceit. Unions that are constantly afraid that employers are out to destroy them are not encouraged to behave in an enlightened and co-operative way. If employers want responsible unionism, they must demonstrate that they deserve it; this is a lesson that the unions must also learn. Better industrial relations do not mean that management and unions must always see eye to eye, but they should have mutual respect and an honest appreciation of one another's responsibilities.

Unfortunately, in spite of the considerable improvement in industrial relations in the post-war period, unions and employers trust each other too little. Unions are not prepared to accept the notion that workers should have the freedom to join or not to join a union; if they do not obtain a 'union shop' agreement, they deliberately and with calculation exploit every grievance, real and imagined, to the utmost possible degree in order to prove that the price of voluntary unionism is extremely high.

It should be recognised by all concerned that a trade union that is democratic is likely to be vigorous in its collective bargaining. If it is responsive to its members' demands, it will inevitably be an aggressive defender of what they conceive to be their rights. It does not follow, however, as some trade unionists and some academics seem to believe, that a democratic union must be an irresponsible union.* Rank-and-file trade unionists are capable of recognising the hard facts of a bargaining situation and they can

* See Clark Kerr, *Unions and Union Leaders of their Own Choosing*, Institute of Industrial Relations. University of California.

be brought to see their responsibilities to the public, as well as to
their own self-interest, if they are given the type of leadership that
they respect.

Democracy is not antithetical to sound, responsible leadership,
but it requires leaders of superior ability and integrity, not the
type who are usually found in a bureaucratic, dictatorial organisation. There is no reason why in the future American unions should
not find men who are capable of leading in a genuinely democratic
fashion as they have done in the past. If they do not find leaders of
this stature, then none of the measures to make unions more democratic will mean very much, since, in the last resort, democracy
is a matter of the personal morality of both leaders and led.

IV

Corruption

The setting

No aspect of industrial relations in the United States is more astonishing to the onlooker from overseas than the picture of corruption and racketeering which, from time to time, is luridly exposed by the Courts and congressional committees. The problem is by no means a new one, but the growth in the size of the unions, the increase in their power and influence, and the accumulation of enormous sums in welfare funds, set up by collective agreements, has proved tempting to union leaders of weak moral fibre, and to racketeers seeking profitable fields of activity.

There can be no doubt in the mind of anyone reading the report of the hearings held by a sub-committee of the Senate Committee on Labour and Public Welfare that the investigations have rendered a signal public service. It may, however, be questioned whether the impression created – that the problem is solely one of the venality of trade union leaders – is valid. This is not merely a matter of political justice; it is of fundamental significance to the way in which the problem is to be tackled.

Corruption is deeply embedded in the political, social and commercial life of America, and so far it has not been possible to root it out. In these circumstances it would be truly surprising if the unions, which necessarily operate within the sphere of business and politics, had not been infected. Indeed, it might well be claimed that the unions, in spite of the much-publicised activities of the leaders of certain organisations, have a remarkably good record of clean government.

Union corruption can be divided into three types, though there are no clear dividing lines between them. There is, first, a whole

143

area of activities, not strictly criminal, which involve unethical practices, such as engaging in business deals which create a conflict of interest, investing union money in such a way as to benefit friends, using an expense account to live in an opulent style, drawing excessively high salaries for services of little value to the members. The second type of corruption is where the border line between morally dubious practices and unlawful behaviour is clearly crossed. This may amount to peculation of a trivial kind, or to the diversion of spectacular sums of the union's money into private hands; but it is plain theft, however cleverly it may be disguised. The third kind of corruption that occurs is that which involves the employer or an outside agency. Here the loss sustained by the members may be small when union leaders receive expensive presents from employers, or it may be large when, in exchange for huge 'kickbacks', their leaders agree to a 'sweetheart' contract which deprives them of wage advances which they could otherwise legitimately expect to secure.*

The internal fight against corruption

The AFL-CIO has tried to deal with the first type of corruption in its ethical codes, to which affiliated organisations are expected to subscribe. The pertinent code states unequivocally that 'a basic ethical principle in the conduct of trade union affairs is that no responsible trade union official should have a personal financial interest which conflicts with the full performance of his fiduciary duties as a workers' representative'.

This code of conduct is scorned by Mr. Hoffa, leader of the Teamsters' Union, who asks why union leaders should be called upon to behave differently from other sections of the community.† Gifts are an accepted lubricant of the commercial world; business men reward their friends handsomely, and they frequently hold stock and directorships in companies with which they are in com-

---

* 'Sweetheart' contracts are settlements accepted by union leaders at lower rates than employers could be pressed to pay, in exchange for corrupt personal payments.

† The *Select Committee on Improper Activities in the Labor or Management Field*, Report 1417, found that 'James R. Hoffa grossly misused $2,400,000 in the funds of local 299, Joint Council 43, the Michigan Conference of Teamsters. This vast amount of money was dispensed in a wide variety of matters, but the expenses have a common denominator: financial assistance to himself, cronies and friends.'

petition. To the question of why union leaders should be 'holier than thou' the AFL-CIO code replies, because union leaders are in a position of public trust.

'Like public servants, trade union leaders ought to be paid compensation commensurate with their services. But, like public servants, trade union leaders must accept certain limitations upon their private activities which result from the nature of their services.'

To ensure that the standards of behaviour expected of union officials are secured, the AFL-CIO has laid down a code of minimum accounting and financial controls that should be put into practice by all affiliates. If all the measures suggested were in fact put into effect, the problem of corruption would rapidly be brought to an end. Unfortunately, the problem is a stubborn one, and it will not be solved merely by the publication of ethical codes, excellent as they are, though this was clearly a necessary step in the direction of cleaner unionism. The much more difficult task which confronts the leaders of the AFL-CIO in their attempt to root out the evil of corruption is that of enforcing the standards laid down.

The AFL-CIO, like the British T.U.C. but unlike the Dutch, German, and Scandinavian trade union centres, has relatively little power over the way in which unions conduct their internal affairs. The dominant tradition in the American labour movement is that of the absolute autonomy of the affiliated unions. It was for this reason that for many years the AFL made no attempt to oust affiliated unions that were in the grip of gangsters or were led by men who put self-enrichment before their duty to their members. The revelations of the tie-up between underworld elements and the unions made in recent years by various investigating committees, prosecutions in the Courts, and a flood of articles in the Press, brought a pressure to bear on the leaders of the AFL that could hardly be ignored.

Perhaps the most important change, however, was the advent of George Meany to the top position in the AFL, following the death of William Green. Meany, a tough, courageous figure, was determined to unite the labour movement, which had been divided for almost twenty years. The pace of re-unification was, however, being set by Walter Reuther, the puritan leader of the automobile workers, who made clean unionism a condition of the unification.

J

Meany was as well aware as Reuther that the status of the unions in the eyes of the public was at stake, and since his election he has pursued a vigorous campaign against corruption.

Meaney's first attack on union corruption was launched against the gangster-ridden International Longshoremen's Association. The I.L.A. was expelled, and Meany instigated a vigorous campaign to build a new union that would be completely free of the crooks who continued to dominate the I.L.A., even after its erstwhile leader had been sent to jail. The attempt failed, against the refusal of the employers on the New York waterfront to break with the I.L.A., and in face of the perverse loyalty of the rank-and-file members to a union about which they can have had no illusions.

This experience revealed all the difficulties that confronted the AFL-CIO, and it says much for the integrity of Meany and Reuther that they have continued the campaign for clean unionism. Four more unions were eventually indicted by the Executive Board of the AFL-CIO, following revelations of corruption and un-democratic practices. Two unions, the Teamsters' and the Bakery and Confectionery Workers', were finally expelled for failing to clean house.

Expulsion is the last resort of the AFL-CIO, and it at once exposes the weakness of the central organisation. Once a union is disaffiliation, the AFL-CIO can exercise no further authority over it. The utmost it can do is to promote a rival union – the experience of the I.L.A. expulsion indicates that this may not be a successful endeavour. If it fails, then there is little more that can be done. When the union is massive, occupies a key position, and has a leadership that is securely entrenched, such as the Teamsters', any attempt to establish a rival body would lead to an inter-necine war that could do immense damage to both organisations. It would be a war of attrition that the AFL-CIO could only win if it had unanimous support from all its affiliates and their members, from employers, from federal and local governmental and other agencies, and from organs of public opinion. It can be well appreciated why the AFL-CIO hesitates to begin such an adventure. The cleaning up of an organisation as powerful as the Teamsters' is beyond the powers of the AFL-CIO; it must be done by the agencies of the government and the Courts.

It is interesting to note that in their counter-attacks on the AFL-

CIO the leaders of the Teamsters' Union have looked for and found allies in strange quarters. Because they are destructively militant, against the AFL-CIO, against the Government, against good employers and harmonious industrial relations, they have attracted the support of the Trotskyite sect of the American socialist movement and numerous other ex-socialists for whom the lure of high living and power has been irresistible. They have even won allies among left-wing socialists in Britain. The Editorial Board of the magazine *Trade Union Affairs* published in its first issue an article calculated to attract support for Hoffa, who was depicted as a union leader fighting valiantly against a vicious campaign launched by a right-wing Government and capitalist employers prepared to stop at nothing to halt a militant trade union and destroy its leadership. The same issue of this magazine contains an article by an official of the International Longshoremen's Union, which was expelled by the CIO as it was Communist controlled.

In the case of the small Bakery and Confectionery Workers' Union, a new organisation has effectively taken over the member-ship of the old union, following its expulsion from the AFL-CIO. New leaders have been elected and a new constitution, far more democratic than the previous one, has been adopted. The United Textile Workers', after a period of suspension by the AFL-CIO, reorganised and has now been declared free from the cor-rupt elements that previously held it in thrall. The fourth union, the International Union of Operating Engineers, which was described in the interim report of the Senate Committee on Im-proper Activities in the Labour or Management Field as 'an ugly example of ruthless domination of working men and women through violence, intimidation and other dictatorial practices', has not been expelled from the AFL-CIO, but it has not yet been given a clean bill of health, and it is not clear whether effective reforms have been carried out.

These examples demonstrate that it is possible for the AFL-CIO to exercise a salutary influence on the affairs of affiliated unions, but that its powers are limited by the willingness of mem-bers of the unions to support a drive to rid them of corrupt leaders. It may be doubted, however, whether the AFL-CIO would have been able to achieve these results without the investigatory work and searing reports of the Senate committees.

Governmental control

Union leaders have been reluctant to accept that some new legislation was required to give additional protection and support union
members against the depredations of unscrupulous officers. The
Labour Management Reporting and Disclosure Act has been the
subject of bitter criticism from both AFL-CIO leaders and Mr.
Hoffa and his associates.

Now that an Act to secure the reporting and disclosure of the
financial activities of union officials has been passed, the question
still to be answered is whether this will prove effective. Here one
is brought up against a major difficulty, endemic in the American
system of society, the problem of law enforcement. No country
has more legal regulation of trade unions and industrial relations
than the United States. Yet, in spite of the pervasive extension of
the law, corruption, boss control, and sectional irresponsibility
appear to be more widespread than in any of the European countries with a comparable degree of labour organisation. If the laws
were fully carried out and union constitutions were properly respected, the situation would undoubtedly be very different, but
unfortunately compliance is extremely difficult to achieve.

The division of responsibility between state and federal authorities for the punishment of crime – inevitable under a federal system
– has long been recognised as a handicap to effective law enforcement in the United States. It has been notoriously difficult to obtain
convictions against 'racketeers'. This is partly because the crimes
they commit are technically difficult to prove, and because both
federal and state authorities are often reluctant to press home an
indictment for fear of social and political consequences.

It is unfortunately true that during the Roosevelt-Truman period
of Democratic rule in the White House there was, judging by post-
Truman figures of indictments against union officials, a reluctance
to prosecute. In the period from 1945 to 1952 only five cases involving union officials and corruption were filed by the Department
of Justice. From 1952 to 1955 the number was seventy, involving
149 individuals, but only twenty-two convictions were obtained,
involving forty-six persons.

The federal authorities in recent years have tackled the problem
with greater energy, but the much more difficult task is to galvanise

state authorities into action. 'It is upon state and local prosecuting agencies, police, and Courts that the major responsibility for the detection, apprehension, prosecution and punishment of offenders rests,' pointed out the Report of the Kefauver Committee, which did much to uncover the way in which gangsters had obtained control of the unions in the port of New York and elsewhere.*

The Federal Government is, unfortunately, almost powerless to compel state and local governments to carry out their responsibilities. As the American Bar Association has emphasised, the Federal Government cannot compel state and local authorities to remove law-enforcement officials who have connived at criminal activities.†
It cannot prevent gangsters and racketeers from exerting influence on responsive political machines. Nor can it ensure that local police, prosecuting agencies, and judges are efficient, determined, and free from undesirable influences and the misguided tolerance of the corrupt, venal, and morally weak elements who prey upon the public, workers, and employers.

The situation which faces the United States in this respect springs out of her history, the size of the country, the variations in economic conditions, and the diverse origins of the population, and from her expanding physical and technological frontier. Out of this complex has come an ambivalent attitude towards society and the law. On the one hand, the overwhelming need to impose a system of law and order on a conglomeration of diverse, individualistic, pragmatic human beings is recognised as vital to the survival of the society; on the other hand, there is deep resentment at being cribbed, cabined, and confined by legal regulation.

The forces generated by these two desires naturally pull in opposing directions and set up their own counterpoise. The inevitable response to the extension of the law is an extension of lawbreaking. To break the law without getting caught is often perversely admired, and the agencies of law enforcement have frequently to work in an atmosphere of indifference, if not opposition. The person who is able to cut corners, to break through, to get things done – these expressions are often euphemisms for, at worst, breaking the law,

* *Organized Crime in Interstate Commerce,* Third Interim Report of the Special U.S. Senate Committee to Investigate Crime in Interstate Commerce, 82nd Congress, 1st Sess., Washington, 1951.
† American Bar Association, *Organized Crime and Law Enforcement,* New York, 1952.

and, at best, evading it in the spirit if not in the letter – is acclaimed as 'smart', and deserving of success. Before clean unionism can be expected there must be a change in the general attitude of the American public towards the law and its enforcement.

Employer attitudes

The efforts that are now being made to clean up the unions will not be successful unless they are supported by comparable efforts among the employers. If employers continue to offer bribes, pay 'kickbacks', and provide, through intermediaries, lavish expenditures for the purpose of corrupting and suborning union officials, the problem will not be solved. It would be unfair to tar all business men with this brush, but it is apparent that a few employers are only too eager to use criminals, to spend money without regard for the morality of what they are doing, and many make no bones about their preference for a union leader of James Hoffa's type to one like Walter Reuther.

The hatred felt towards Walter Reuther by some business men is astonishing in its vehemence. Such bitter feelings towards a man who, by every test, is not only a union leader of absolute probity but also has an outstanding record of intelligent, responsible leadership is in itself a sign of moral sickness. Opposition to the ideas of Mr. Reuther is perfectly understandable, and, indeed, in a democratic society it is desirable that there should be opposition, but to indicate a preference for unions that are notoriously corrupt is to let prejudice blind moral judgement to a degree that offers little hope of a rapid improvement in the ethical standards of these employers.*

The unhelpful and unreasonable stubbornness of some American employers was harshly revealed by the attitude of the National Association of Manufacturers and the Chambers of Commerce towards the Bill that was originally promoted by Senator Kennedy to eliminate corrupt practices. Because the Bill placed a legal obligation on employers spending more than $5,000 a year

---

* Reuther is looked upon by right-wing Republicans, especially from Texas and California, as a rabid socialist. By British standards Reuther would be a progessive Conservative. He is not in favour of nationalisation but he is in favour of effective competition and he looks to the Government to interfere when, in his opinion, this is required in the interests of his members and the public.

on activities intended to influence or affect employees in the exercise of rights guaranteed under the National Labour Relations Act as amended, or by the Railway Labour Act – to file similar information to that called for from the unions – it was bitterly opposed. The Bill certainly had flaws in drafting that could be interpreted as imposing an onerous burden upon employers, but it was not this fact so much as the complete refusal to admit of any interference with the freedom of employers to behave as they may choose which determined this opposition. It is at once obvious to any objective observer that it is just as important to prevent employers from spending money on bribing or otherwise influencing trade union leaders in the conduct of their duties as it is to deter union leaders from demanding or taking unlawful payments.

The moral climate of industry varies quite considerably, but it would appear that the industries that are composed of relatively small employers, generally operating in highly competitive local markets, are those that show corruption at its worst. It is difficult to imagine one of the major manufacturing companies, today, resorting to the kind of bribery and blackmail that sometimes goes on at other levels. Small firms are far more vulnerable than large enterprises to the kind of pressure that can be exerted by a powerful union. Thus, the source of corruption in the trucking and longshore industries has much to do with their structure and manner of organisation. These industries lend themselves to exploitation by gangsters, who, once established, become very difficult to dislodge.

In their loyalty to discredited officers, many truck drivers show how low down in their scale of moral judgement they hold the conversion of union funds for the personal benefit of their leaders, and the employment of gangsters and convicted criminals. The attitude expressed in this kind of statement, 'Why shouldn't Jimmy do something for himself and his friends? Everybody else does, and so would I if I had the chance,' is widespread among Hoffa's members. It is this type of outlook which is the source of the Teamsters' leader's formidable strength; it is, at the same time, a measure of the size of the problem that has to be overcome before American unionism can hope to escape from corruption.

It is frequently suggested that one of the factors causing American unions to become corrupt is their lack of a social philosophy and the decline in their missionary zeal. When Gompers defeated the Socialists, in the decades before the First World War, he saved American unions from adopting an alien political philosophy at the expense of directing their entire energies towards the securing of higher wages and better working conditions. The rejection of social unionism in favour of business unionism, it is argued, necessarily involved embracing the ethics of business – elevating materialism, maximising the return on the dollar, and putting acquisitiveness before brotherhood or the achievement of a socially superior society.

This type of analysis of what is wrong with American unions grossly overweights the adverse effects of the pursuit of sectional interests. American unions perhaps focus their attention more aggressively on the bread-and-butter interests of their members, but they are much concerned with wider social and economic factors. It must, however, be admitted that American unions have now reached a state of development where they are faced with a serious challenge. When the wages of millions of workers were extremely low, when millions of workers had no jobs, and the vast majority of them were not even organised, the unions had tremendous giants to slay. They had objectives that transcended any narrow concept of personal, materialist ambition; they were fighting for social ideals, for the betterment of man and his society. Now that these things have been largely achieved, where, the question may be asked, are the unions to obtain the moral dynamic that is required to defeat corrupting cynicism? Is it not vital that they should re-examine their basic philosophy?

Corruption and society

The general absence of corruption in the trade unions of Britain, Germany, Holland, and Scandinavia is frequently cited as proof of the significance of a motivating social philosophy. It is true that European trade unionists are more conscious of political factors than their American counterparts, but it is difficult to believe that their social motivation is in itself an adequate explanation of the absence of corruption. It should not be forgotten that there are trade unions in the Middle East, Africa, Asia, Latin America, and even parts of Europe, where corruption is endemic in spite of the fact that the unions are intensely motivated by political and social factors. Corruption certainly has something to do with the social goals of an institution, but the behaviour of union members is not conditioned by their union membership alone. It is a product of the values of the society to which they belong; a union cannot avoid being a mirror of the qualities that are accepted in that society in the round. It would, then, seem that there is no absolute reason why American unions should be faced with a problem of corruption other than the fact that corruption is a problem of American society.

It does not follow from this conclusion, however, that American unions are not faced with the task of changing the attitude of their members towards the goals of unionism. If American society as a whole is to break free from corruption it will have to lay more emphasis on the responsibility of the individual, in his vocational relationships, to maintain high ethical standards. In union terms, this means that trade union leaders must be both responsive to the needs of the members and responsible to the public interest. The objectives of American unions must, therefore, be more and more concerned with the problems of their members in their full social setting. A number of American unions have, of course, long been deeply concerned about the broader questions of economics, education, racial segregation, housing, and community services; others, however, look upon such responsibilities with cynicism. Somehow the average member has to be convinced that his union is of sufficient importance to warrant his placing it high on his list of social interests. At present it is often extremely low on this list, and this fact is to no small extent responsible for the present situation.

'All that is necessary for the forces of evil to win in the world is for enough good men to do nothing.' Edmund Burke's classic reminder of a vital truth has never been more clearly demonstrated than in the United States. Unfortunately, in the choice between the type of leadership offered by James Hoffa and that offered by Walter Reuther, it may well be that a majority of American workers as well as employers would prefer the former. This would not be a deliberate vote for corruption – that would not be looked upon with favour – but it would be a vote in support of the narrow concept of bread-and-butter unionism that was favoured with good cause by Samuel Gompers. The main difference between what Hoffa stands for and what Gompers stood for, apart from standards of personal probity, is that nowadays the butter needs to be spread on more thickly. We have, however, learned during the past quarter of a century that bread, even with a lot of butter, does not make an adequate diet for a healthy body.

Hoffa is said to have stated that he 'fears a guy who does not want to make money'. The suggestion that Reuther is intent on compelling American workers to accept alien concepts of society – usually socialism or communism is suggested – is a potent anti-dote to the criticism that Hoffa stands for things that are evil in American society. How can the making of money be evil? Is this not the primary purpose of economic activity? Why should the unions concern themselves with matters that are of interest to 'eggheads'? There can be little doubt that this appeal evokes a heady response from a society in which many of its members are ill-educated, narrowly experienced, and feel insecure. The fight for the soul of the American labour movement will not easily be won for enlightenment and the nobler aspects of life, but the response to the McClellan Committee's request for information about un-democratic and corrupt union practices, which came in letters from thousands of rank-and-file members, at once suggests that there is a latent hunger for honest, democratic unionism that could be en-couraged by the resolute leadership of good men.

Although attention has been focused in this section on the prob-lem of corruption, it is well, however, to remember that the majority of American unions are honestly administered; that it is the leaders of the AFL-CIO who have made a stand against corruption, risked their own careers, and brought the threat of disintegration upon their organisation rather than bow before the evil that menaces the moral status of the American labour movement.

Labour Management Reporting and Disclosure Act, 1959

The general purpose of the Act is to make it obligatory for union officers and employers to disclose and report certain financial trans-actions and administrative practices, to prevent national union leaders from abusing their power, to protect members by estab-lishing and enforcing standards and procedures with the respect to the election and removal of union officers.

The Act lays down a Bill of Rights of union members. This

section of the Act seeks to secure for union members equal rights to nominate candidates and to vote in union elections and to attend and participate in meetings; freedom of speech and assembly; no increase in contributions or assessments without a ballot vote; no limitation of the right of a union member to enforce his rights by instituting legal proceedings.

Under section 2 of the Act every union must file a copy of its constitution with the Secretary of Labour. Each union is required to file annual financial reports containing information specified. Individual officers, employers and labour consultants are required to file reports on any financial transactions involving a 'conflict of interest' and expenditures for the purpose of influencing employees in the exercise of their protected rights of representation.

All reports are public and the union must make the records necessary to verify the reports available to their members.

Every union which assumes supervisory control over a subordinate body must file a report with the Secretary of Labour within thirty days of assuming such a trusteeship. Trusteeships might only be invoked for specified reasons.

The Act requires union officers to be elected directly by secret ballot or by delegates who have been elected by secret vote. In elections the rights of members must be fully respected. An election may be challenged by a union member who suspects that his rights have been violated; if after exhaustion of internal remedies he is not satisfied he may complain to the Secretary of Labour, who is empowered to investigate, and if he believes that a violation has recurred he may bring an action in a Federal Court to set aside the election, remove an officer, and supervise fresh elections.

The Act prohibits Communists and felons convicted of enumerated crimes from serving as union officers, labour consultants and officers of employers organisations for five years after termination of membership of the Communist Party or conviction or imprisonment unless citizenship rights have been restored.

The Secretary of Labour is provided with authority to make an investigation whenever he deems this to be necessary in order to determine whether any person has violated or is about to violate the provisions of the Act.

The Labour Management Reporting and Disclosure Act also contains other sections relating to the prohibition of secondary boycotts, and organisational and recognition picketing where another union is the lawfully recognised bargaining agent.

It is too early yet to say whether the Act will achieve the aims of its sponsors. Much will depend upon the vigour of the Secretary of Labour, the readiness of the Courts to move swiftly and effectively and the willingness of the unions to co-operate with the authorities to make the law effective.

When all the circumstances are taken into account the case for the new Act was strong. With Mr. Arthur Goldberg (the man who was responsible for drafting the AFL-CIO ethical codes, which, in effect, form the substance of the Act) as President Kennedy's Secretary of Labour, the chances that the new law will be effectively enforced should be extremely good. Unfortunately, the Act was passed too late to deal with some major transgressors, and it is unlikely to have much effect on the position of Mr. Hoffa, since he is almost certain to behave with circumspection in the future. He now enjoys undisputed power in his union and he is hardly likely to invite further criticism by deliberately flouting the new law.

V

Wage Bargaining and the Control of Inflation

THE trends of development which have significantly affected the pattern of union growth as well as the quality of union democracy and the efficiency and honesty of union government have been felt equally profoundly in the collective bargaining activities of the unions. Bargaining is becoming more centralised, more complex, and, from the point of view of economic welfare, more significant than ever before.

America has a much more competitive economy than Britain; competition is sustained by a vigorous natural urge to make money, and to be highly successful in business is a more compelling incentive than it is on this side of the Atlantic. Antagonism to monopoly is deep-rooted and has been made effective by laws directed against the elimination of competition for over seventy years.

The aggressive business atmosphere in the United States has produced a system of industrial relations in which collective bargaining is a fierce unrelenting battle between two sides both bent on squeezing the other as hard as possible. There is nothing soft or flabby about industrial relations in the United States; the climate of opinion is too harsh to permit the type of easy-going relations which by and large exist in Britain.

In order to protect their members from the relentless drive and determination of American management to produce more efficiently, trade unions in America have developed collective bargaining as an instrument of job regulation at the plant level further than unions in any other country. This has made possible the development of grievance arbitration which goes well beyond what is normal practice in Europe.*

* Sumner H. Slichter, James J. Healy, E. Robert Livernash, *The Impact of Collective Bargaining on Management*, Brookings Institution, 1960.

By comparison with British or European standards American union contracts also cover a far wider range of issues. For example, it is rare in Europe for industrial pensions, health benefits, and lay-off compensation to be the subject of collective bargaining. Where these benefits are provided other than through the state, which is the normal practice in Europe, they have been introduced by welfare-conscious employers who are anxious to set high employment standards. There is in Europe a conflict of opinion on the wisdom of negotiating employer-provided welfare services, on the grounds that they create a considerable inequity between employment in the more and less prosperous industries and between more and less efficient employees. There has, however, been a tendency in Britain to follow the American lead and to develop a system of private benefits over and above those provided by the state system of social insurance.

It is in the field of wage policy that the most interesting similarities and differences arise. In Europe, collective bargaining tends to be far more centralised than in America; agreements are commonly negotiated on an industry-wide scale. There are signs, however, of a distinct trend towards industry-wide bargaining in the United States. To a large extent wages are already determined in the steel, coal, meat-packing, and railroad industries on an industry-wide basis. Recently, developments in the automobile industry, airlines, and trucking have been pushing these groups in the same direction.

The trend towards larger units of collective bargaining is inexorably being brought about by the development of modern technology, allied to the softening of price competition among major manufacturers. As the capital-labour ratio rises, the costs of stoppages and slow-downs become much higher, and it grows increasingly more imperative that expensive equipment should be used fully. Most industrialists who are placed in a relatively weak position to resist wage demands under conditions of full employment are showing signs of preferring to join their rivals in an endeavour to meet the claims of the unions on as broad a front as possible, rather than fight individually. So long as they do not face higher labour costs than their rivals they do not mind wages rising and, if necessary, prices too. It used to be the unions who were in favour of industry-wide bargaining; now it is the employers, and the unions are rather afraid that the growth of collaboration between employers will prevent them from using the whipsaw technique and so curb their bargaining strength.*

Anti-trust legislation imposes limitations to the development of a more corporate form of economic structure, but the trend of developments in modern times has tended to soften the degree of competition in the American economy. It is unlikely that either business men or trade unionists would support more vigorous anti-trust policies than prevail. And a Democratic Congress and President are hardly likely to seek the repeal of the Fair Trade Practices Act or refuse to permit unions to enter into agreements covering a wider area than the plant. There are few signs that the American public, business men or unions are prepared to reverse the trends which are tending to reduce the competitive vigour of industry and industrial relations. It is, therefore, possible to see that although America is a more competitive society than Britain, the direction of its development is towards the creation of a more socially responsive system.

With the virtual abandonment of socialism by Western European labour movements and the growing similarity between their economic structures and the American, there is a rising interest in the achievements of unions on the American side of the Atlantic. The development in American collective bargaining which has perhaps aroused the greatest interest overseas has been the annual improvement factor combined with the cost-of-living escalator pioneered by the United Automobile Workers' Union, and the long-term contracts associated with it. This development, in Europe as in America, has been thought to offer a possible way of linking wage increase to rises in productivity, without incurring the danger of strikes at regular intervals, and a method of preventing wage costs from rising at an inflationary rate. Whatever their advantages, agreements of this type have not proved to be a counter to the tendency for wages to rise faster than output under conditions of full employment and a high rate of economic growth.

---

* This development in the structure of collective bargaining is closely bound up with the trend towards administrative centralisation discussed in Chapter I.

The problem of creeping inflation

The persistent tendency for wages and prices to spiral upwards in the past decade has aroused the most vigorous debate in the field of economics, at both the theoretical and the public-policy level, since the great controversy in the 1930s about the way to escape from mass unemployment. No one wishes to return to the old situation, but the pressures of unions, business men and politicians has produced a situation with many serious and disturbing consequences.*

Inflation of a moderate kind may bring more advantages than disadvantages to a country like America, as Sumner Slichter has cogently argued, but constantly rising prices are difficult to live with under any circumstances. Even those who have benefited from the inflation during the past twenty years have found that the continuous adjustments which are required impose a burden that is hard to bear. In spite of rapidly rising real wages, the wives of wage earners feel they are fighting a losing battle with prices. Most people, in all income brackets, tend to be victims of the money illusion; they find difficulty in discounting the rise in prices that they know from experience will occur when incomes rise as fast as they have done in modern times, and they raise their level of committed income to a point which puts them under a strain as prices go up. It gives the puritanical satisfaction to point this out, but the less austere gain no comfort from the fact being drawn to their attention; they prefer stable prices.

Inflation affects not only the distribution of income; it also plays havoc with welfare schemes, and the financing of educational, cultural, and public services becomes a formidable problem as costs continuously rise. As a political issue, rising prices occupy a position of major importance. They were responsible, as much as any other cause, except perhaps unemployment, for the defeat of the Democrats in 1952, and for the defeat of the Republicans in 1958. In Britain, it was the failure of the Labour Government to prevent prices from rising, year after year, that sent it to defeat in 1951.

In the light of this experience, it is not necessary to stress the importance of inflation as a social problem. It is necessary, how-

* *Wages, Prices, Profits and Productivity.* The American Assembly, 1959, Columbia University.

ever, to put the problem, as it faces the people of the United States, in perspective by comparing the degree to which prices have risen in other countries. On this basis, America has not been much afflicted by inflation. In Britain, Holland, and the Scandinavian countries, for example, prices have risen at more than twice the annual average of the United States; in many other countries the rise has been much faster. However important it might be to prevent inflation in America, which has developed a minor balance of payments problem, it is much more important in countries such as Britain, Holland, and Sweden, which have a major balance of payments problem.

Much as inflation is feared by the American public, high unemployment and a stagnant economy are probably feared even more. It is almost certain that President Kennedy would not have been elected in 1960 had not the fear of depression stimulated a huge Democratic vote in the industrial cities of America.

Any President bent on raising the level of employment and the rate of economic growth is faced by a very difficult situation. If fiscal and monetary policies are adopted to achieve these results, the danger of inflation and of increasing the outflow of gold from America is very real. Politically, it is impossible to do nothing when unemployment rises to a high level and evidence accumulates that America's lead in the economic marathon with Russia and her satellites is being reduced. In these circumstances, the role of the trade unions is inevitably crucial.

Are the unions responsible for inflation?

It is widely believed, in every country, that the inflation which has been experienced in the post-war years has been due to the power of organised labour more than to any other factor. The unions have been castigated for pushing wages up at a rate that exceeds the pace at which the output of goods and services is increasing. Whatever the truth of this allegation, the curbing of union power in the field of collective bargaining has everywhere become a major issue of public policy.

The unions in America have come in for a large share of the blame for the creation of excess monetary demand, since they are responsible for bringing pressure to bear upon employers, who are then faced with the alternatives of agreeing to the wage increase

K

demanded, and meeting it by increasing efficiency, reducing profit margins, or raising prices, or of refusing the unions' request and enduring a strike. In recent years, employers have become more and more reluctant to face strikes, and the number of stoppages caused by wage demands has tended to fall in America and in most other advanced countries. Under conditions of full employment governments have tended to encourage employers to settle disputes at inflationary wage levels rather than fight prolonged battles; and by their economic policies they have assisted employers to take the easiest way out of their problems by passing on increased costs to the consumer.

American governments have been tougher than most European governments in opposing inflation, but they have not found the task of preventing price increases an easy one. Reducing spending in the face of rising costs is a very difficult thing for governments to achieve; it is no more popular than raising taxes. The net effect of this situation is that American governments have found the task of balancing their budgets extremely difficult, and they have tended to accept a certain degree of inflation as inevitable.

Thus whatever pressures unions exert they are only one factor in a chain of events that requires the participation of others before the full effect of an inflationary increase in prices occurs.

As we noted in Chapter II, only about one-third of the employees in non-supervisory and professional categories are members of trade unions. This membership is, further, highly concentrated in the manufacturing, construction, mining, and transport industries. It is in these areas that collective agreements predominate and in which the unions exercise most influence. From this situation it might be expected that the cost of labour, and therefore prices, would have risen most rapidly in the manufacturing sector of the American economy. This, however, does not turn out to be entirely true, because it is in this sector of the economy that productivity rises most rapidly; wage costs per unit of product did not, in fact, rise in manufacturing in the United States between 1952 and 1956. Wage costs tended to rise in 1957 because productivity was cut back during the recession, but the slowing down of wage increases in 1958, together with the great increase in productivity that accompanied the recovery, checked this increase.

Why, then, have prices continued to rise? Unfortunately, wage costs have risen in the service and ancillary industries, which are not capable of raising their productivity at the same rate of advance as the manufacturing sector. Then, in the manufacturing sector itself, there has been a vast increase in the employment of research, design, administrative, sales, public relations, and other non-immediately productive workers. The costs of the expanded use of these technical and professional personnel have risen with the rise in demand for their services.

Thus we find that it is in the weakly organised sectors of the American economy that labour costs have risen most; and the rise has been brought about, in the main, not by union pressure but by the competitive bidding of employers in a relatively tight labour market. It would be foolish to suggest that collective bargaining has had no effect in generalising wage advances made in the high-productivity sectors of the economy, but the main responsibility for this development is to be found in deeper social and economic factors.

The cost of controlling inflation

It is apparent from previous experience that money wages will rise, whether there are strong unions or not, under conditions of excess demand. If the problem were merely one of checking prices from rising, then it would be relatively easy to resolve. The real difficulty arises when the attempt is made to achieve two other goals at the same time – namely full employment and a high level of economic growth.

Unemployment in the United States has always been at a higher figure than in Britain, Holland, and the Scandinavian countries. The figures generally quoted are not strictly comparable, since the methods of measurement employed are different in each country, but even when this has been taken into account unemployment in America is still higher than has become normal in Britain and Europe.* Since production has also risen more rapidly in the United States, and money wages have not gone up so fast, prices have risen less. This relative advantage has not made the price

* The higher American figure is due in part to structural features in the economy, the size and variation in the country, much greater seasonal effects than in Britain and the large floating juvenile working population.

increases, which have occurred, or the unemployment, easy to accept as inevitable consequences of economic policy.

Unemployment was allowed to go up in the United States in 1958 to 7 per cent; industrial production fell from its 1957 peak by 16 per cent. The losses incurred by the check to inflation in the European countries were not so dramatic. In Britain, for example, unemployment rose to only 2·5 per cent, and industrial production fell by only 4 per cent.

Organised labour in both America and Britain has been a severe critic of the counter-inflationary policies of their governments and central banks. In the United States, the Federal Reserve Board was harshly criticised for seeking to damp down the investment boom by raising the discount rate and the administration for failing to inject a stimulant into the economy by way of a tax cut and increase in public spending, when it began to be apparent that the anti-inflationary measures had been effective. If the view is taken that the social losses incurred by idle capacity and relatively high unemployment exceed those generated by a moderate degree of inflation, then the demands of the trade unions make perfectly good sense.

The difficulty, however, of this point of view soon becomes apparent when the recovery begins and prices start to rise. It is easy during a recession, when attention shifts from rising prices to unemployment, to win support for the view that a depression is far more dangerous than inflation and ought not to be risked at any cost. When the recovery gets into high gear, however, it is the rise in prices that becomes all-important.

The choice, then, that would seem to lie before America, and for that matter Britain and other countries, is between using effectively the classical, but clearly rather clumsy, instruments of fiscal and monetary policies alone or in using them in conjunction with wage, price, and other controls over capital and consumption expenditures, or of continuing to tolerate the losses and handicaps to economic growth and stability of inflation.

A national wages policy

The American labour movement has traditionally not favoured wage controls in peacetime, though it has accepted far-reaching intervention with free collective bargaining in wartime. In this respect, the American trade unions have been less hostile to the introduction of governmental controls than the British labour movement, which would not agree to the determination of wages by an agency of the government even in wartime. It is true that in Britain strikes were outlawed and that unions and employers had to submit their disputes to a National Arbitration Tribunal, whose awards were legally binding, but there was no control over wage increases that were agreed upon by consent.

If the American trade unions insist – now the Democrats are in the White House – upon the government following a policy that will reduce unemployment to well under 4 per cent and, at the same time, substantially increase public expenditure, then they will also be faced by a problem of inflation again. It is not only pressure from the unions that is likely to push the American economy towards inflation in the future. The rapid increase in production in the Soviet Union is encouraging politicians and public opinion to demand a faster rate of economic growth. Defence expenditures are unlikely to fall far, and the demand for high profits will hardly subside. Taken together, the pressures generated by these forces are almost certain to produce substantial price rises once the economy is again running in high gear.

There is then bound to be a public demand for steps to be taken to curb the rise in the cost of living, and something will have to be done to satisfy the political pressures that these public feelings will create. Unless the government is prepared to follow the course now condemned by the unions and the Democrats, an alternative method of maintaining price stability will have to be devised. In the circumstances envisaged it is quite probable that, after talks between the government, employers, and the unions, some form of machinery for controlling the rate of wage increases will be established. The trend in this direction is also likely to be fostered by the growing authority of the AFL-CIO and the increasing desire of the unions to behave responsibly.

Nevertheless, the chances of success for a national approach to the wages problem are, if past experience is any guide, likely to be slim. An idea of the value of a national wages policy as a method of preventing inflation may be gained from an examination of the results achieved in the United States in the Second World War and the Korean War and in several European countries during the past decade. The most thorough-going of the peacetime experiments has been conducted in Holland; the Scandinavian countries have also adopted similar ideas, but have not carried them quite so far. Britain also tried for two years to prevent an excessive rise in wages by persuading the unions to enter into a voluntary pact to limit wage increases only to situations where there had been a clear rise in productivity, or there was a need to correct a manifest inequity.

The outstanding result of these bold ventures in economic planning and control of collective bargaining has been a failure to prevent inflation.* In every one of the European countries concerned, prices have gone up during the post-war period at a much faster pace than in the United States.

It should be added that, during the period of the Korean war, in spite of a Wage Stabilisation Board, America was no more successful than other countries in keeping wages and prices steady.

The pressure of demand for labour generated in the countries with national wage policies was such that both unions and employers constantly sought to limit the effectiveness of the controls to which they had formally given their support. In every country with a national wages policy there developed the phenomenon aptly called by the Swedes the wage drift. That is to say, actual wages were always well above the level formally agreed upon under the wage plans.

A similar situation occurred in Britain during the period of wage restraint. The unions loyally agreed to their part of the bargain, that they would not push for higher wages except in the special circumstances allowed for; they could not prevent employers from offering to raise wages or their members from accepting such offers. With full order books, employers were willing to pay more to obtain the labour that they required by providing special bonuses, more overtime at higher rates, easy piece-prices under incentive schemes, upgrading and personal-merit awards. These additions to the pay packet were not the fruit of national negotiations with the unions, but the result of local, often personal, bargaining that occurred at the places of work. It was thus impossible to stop wages from rising without introducing far-reaching controls, which Ameri-

* For a detailed examination of this experience, see my *National Wages Policy in War and Peace*, Allen and Unwin, London, 1958.

can experience during the Wage Stabilisation Board period showed are extremely difficult to administer effectively over any lengthy period without inducing revolt.

From this analysis of likely events and the probable outcome, it would seem almost certain that America will have difficulty in avoiding some degree of inflation. How much inflation will be determined by the level of unemployment that is found to be politically tolerable. It has been shown by experience during the post-war years that when unemployment falls below 4 per cent the conditions in the labour market lead to a rate of wage increase that outpaces productivity.* On the other hand, when the demand for labour falls and unemployment moves up above this figure, the rate of wage increase is slowed down to a speed that can be matched by output. This level of unemployment, however, appears to be politically intolerable.

A non-inflationary level of demand might be more acceptable if unemployment compensation were more adequate. This would require changes in the financing of this benefit, much higher scales, and a longer duration. However, even if a better system of unemployment compensation were adopted, it is inevitable that from time to time the authorities would overshoot the mark and get into difficulties with either too much or too little unemployment. It may not be necessary or desirable to erect a massive apparatus like the Wage Stabilisation Board to get out of a situation of this kind, but it would be very much easier to get back into an equilibrium position if both sides of industry would co-operate.

It can be said with certainty that if employers and unions both insist on obtaining the highest money incomes without reference to the effect on the general economic situation and the interests of the wider public, and the government is prepared to allow those demands to be financed, inflation will not be prevented. The price of economic stability is a high degree of responsibility from all concerned. Whether this can be achieved will depend on the pursuit of an effective policy by the White House and Congress and the achievement of a better spirit of industrial relations than at present prevails.

---

* This figure is comparable with a figure of approximately 2 per cent unemployed in the United Kingdom.

VI

Industrial Relations

The climate of industrial relations

THE average amount of time lost by workers employed in American industry through industrial strife during the post-war period has been five or six times as much as that lost by workers employed in Britain. This contrast is even more marked if the comparison is made with Holland or Germany. It is a commonplace for visitors to America from European countries to remark on the apparently much less friendly relations between unions and management in the United States. They are astonished at the virulent criticism that is expressed during industrial disputes, at the apparent readiness of unions and employers to ignore all other interests but their own. What is, perhaps, most paradoxical is that industrial relations in countries with a far less egalitarian social structure than America, and in which trade unions have a strong ideological character, should be less marked by bitter antagonism.

The turbulent history of America is naturally one of the primary reasons why the relations between unions and employers are manifestly more hostile than in Europe. Industrial relations are an expression of the character of a society and they reflect its principal features. The dynamic growth of America was brought about by those elements from the older civilisation of Europe who had been limited by the bonds of social structure, which made for stable but miserable and frustrating conditions, throwing off these restraints in the New World. A new life could be won only by an aggressive, ruthless determination to succeed. Not surprisingly, industrial relations were bloody. Employers who had built vast enterprises by vigorous, driving ability were hardly likely to take kindly to attempts by unions to limit their freedom to hire and fire, and to give orders and have them executed without question. Except in the settled conditions of the older eastern seaboard towns where the pattern of life and the character of industry and trade closely resembled that of Europe, the unions had to fight grimly for the right to organise.

Although trade unions are today clearly well enough established to put their existence and their fundamental right to organise, to bargain, and to strike beyond question of doubt, there are still some employers who refuse to accept this fact. The majority of business men, however, realise that they cannot afford to pay the price of not recognising the existence of the unions; the problem, as most of them see it, is not to get rid of the unions but to curb their demands to limits that are acceptable.

The unions with a history of bitter, violent conflict behind them, a history which has involved having had to battle with the Press, the pulpit, the police, the Courts, Congress, and the President, have been nurtured in the belief that any respect that they might enjoy is to be measured by their power to fight all and sundry. This attitude is still important, but the behaviour of the unions is changing, as the employers, under the conditions of high levels of employment, high rates of economic growth, and technological change, offer less resistance to their claims. The decline of competition in some major areas is also likely to be a significant factor contributing to the softening of the harsh lines of conflict and encouraging collusion to promote common interests.

Given the history and traditions of industrial relations in America, it will be a long time before her unions are as little prone to use the strike as a tactical and strategic weapon in collective bargaining as those in many parts of Europe, but the trend in the United States is in the same downward direction as elsewhere.*

The character of industrial strife

Strikes are extremely difficult social phemonena to classify neatly. Their causes, though often ascribed to some simple factor, such as a demand for higher wages, are usually found upon examination to be extremely complex. In some situations the principal causes will be economic, in others political; in few situations will every-

* A. M. Ross and P. T. Hartman, *Changing Patterns of Industrial Conflict,* John Wiley & Sons, 1960.

body be agreed upon the fundamental thing that he or she is striking for. The strike seems to provide a means of satisfying important psychological needs among groups of workers and will not, necessarily, disappear as wages are raised, even though this is commonly believed. Before strikes can be eliminated it is necessary to find some alternative method of satisfying whatever are the factors causing the strikes.

In a free country it is impossible to eliminate industrial disputes by law, as the evidence of Australian experience overwhelmingly demonstrates; strikes may be successfully regulated and controlled, but any attempt to make them totally disappear is doomed to failure in any but a totalitarian country. Even then, it is an illusion to believe that the absence of strikes is proof of harmonious industrial relations; there are many other ways in which industrial conflict and dissatisfaction will find an outlet.

The contrast between the nature of industrial strife in Britain and America is quite marked. Whereas strikes in the United States occur mainly over changes in the contract, in Britain the agreements are generally concluded without a strike or even the threat of a strike. On the other hand, thousands of strikes occur, where they would never occur in the United States, over the interpretation and carrying out of collective agreements. If the stewards of American unions behaved like their counterparts sometimes do in Britain their organisations would find themselves facing legal actions for damages.

Is it in the contract?

These differences in the pattern of industrial relations are due to fundamental differences in the concept of collective bargaining in the two countries. In Britain, collective agreements are not legally binding contracts; they are, in fact, never referred to as contracts, as is the case in the United States. They are, however, in the nature of gentlemen's agreements and both sides have generally honoured their undertaking with fidelity. Since these agreements are not enforceable in the Courts, there has been no incentive to have them drawn up by lawyers, or to seek to cover every possible facet of industrial relations. Thus, agreements of this kind are not really arbitrable, as is an American collective contract.

The conditions of employment, and the rights and duties of the shop stewards, are more often than not determined by custom and practice rather than by a written agreement. There are many local agreements in effect, but they frequently take the form of verbal undertakings made by management following discussion with the shop stewards. The weakness of the British system lies in the tendency which has developed under full employment for shop stewards to act unconstitutionally and in breach of an agreement to which their union is a party. They suffer no penalty for acting in this way, and their trade union accepts no responsibility for their actions.

All this is very different from the American practice, where 'Is it in the contract?' is the basic question that underlies industrial relations. Since contracts are legal documents, written in precise language that seeks to cover every contingency, with few exceptions they are capable of interpretation by a third party. It has, therefore, been possible to build an elaborate system of grievance arbitration into the American system of industrial relations.

Arbitration

This practice has certain advantages, since each party knows precisely where it stands. If there is a dispute – and there are many disputes which are not settled by the exhaustion of the agreed procedure – they go to the arbitrator for a decision. Unfortunately, one of the weaknesses of this system is that it has tended to generate a legalistic attitude on the part of both parties, who are often more determined to win on a strict interpretation of the contract than to resolve the cause of the problem. The contract may become an end in itself – rather like the Constitution to some people. Where industrial relations are bad both parties are encouraged to take intransigent positions, rather than to iron out their difficulties, in the knowledge that the more vigorous their claim, the more likely they are to obtain something from an arbitrator.

The system of arbitration has virtually eliminated, in America, the 'quickie' strike called by a union to secure the redress of a grievance; it has not entirely eliminated the 'wildcat' strike, which takes the form of a spontaneous combustion when the men walk out in spite of their contract. It is probably impossible to eliminate entirely a sudden flare-up of this kind where there is a bad history of industrial relations, but there are many fewer unofficial strikes in

America than in Britain, which does not have the system of grievance arbitration.

The attitude of the British unions probably has its closest parallel
in the United States in the building trades.* In the construction
industry it is not usual to employ the arbitration system; the unions
and employers both prefer to settle their disputes round the table
rather than shift them to a third party for resolution. The United
Automobile Workers' Union also makes an exception to the normal procedure for settling grievances which arise under the contracts it has signed. This union will not agree to submit to arbitration disputes arising out of changes in production standards, wage
rates for new jobs, the fixing of piece rates, or health and safety
measures. The attitude of the union in this respect is based upon
the belief that arbitration should be strictly confined to interpreting
existing rights; that in the case of establishing new rights the last
arbiter is the strike.

This sharp distinction between one type of dispute that is arbitrable and another that is not may encourage a way of looking at
disputes that promotes tough bargaining, where a question of interest is involved. Members of unions and employers in certain
industries have now become accustomed to the notion that a new
collective agreement cannot be negotiated without a demonstration
on both sides of militancy and a show of proof that they can take
a strike. A threat of a strike is now part of the normal procedure
of bargaining, and even when both sides recognise, as, for example,
in the 1958 negotiations in the automobile industry, that a strike
of any length would be tremendously damaging to both parties, the
motions have to be gone through like the ritual fire dance. The
method of negotiation is to drag out the discussions until the previously fixed strike deadline is almost reached; then, in a feverish
burst of activity, in which the major actors on both sides play
leading roles, if all goes well, agreement is reached in time to get
the men back to work within a few days of their withdrawal from
employment. If worse comes to worst, the stoppage will last until
a significant concession is made by one or both parties. This is not
to suggest that the demands of either party are in any way not
genuine, but that they have become prisoners of their own pattern
of behaviour, which they have now institutionalised as a necessary

* Cf. J. T. Dunlop, *Industrial Relations Systems*, Henry Holt, 1958.

feature of these negotiations. Objectively, nothing could be more absurd; there is no absolute reason why agreements should be reached in this way. They could be arrived at without the building up of an atmosphere that is reminiscent of the pep sessions before a college football game, and that makes a strike something the worker really wants.

Militancy and efficiency

The advantage of the American situation, from a union point of view, is that it makes the role of the union more apparent to the workers. The union seeks to prove that without the contract, won and policed by the union, workers would be at the mercy of the employer and subject to whatever orders he might give, no matter how arbitrary and unfair these were. Every worker must be made to realise this fact, and he must be made to experience the emotions of going on strike to achieve the goals – his goals – for which the union stands.

It is obvious that the justification for industrial stoppages, which may do untold economic damage and probably inflict a loss upon the union members whom they are designed to benefit most, must be founded on less flimsy support than that of merely promoting the cohesion of the organisation. A much more sophisticated and plausible argument that is now advanced by a number of economists is based upon the belief that union pressures compel management to be efficient.* By constantly threatening to go on strike to secure higher wages and better working conditions, unions compel employers to seek ways and means of cutting their labour costs. Thus, there is generated a constant force pushing the employer into installing more labour-saving equipment, into reducing costs in other directions. All of this means that labour productivity is greatly increased over the years. It is alleged that high labour costs, first induced by an acute shortage of labour and now, in effect, continued by the activities of the unions, constitute the principal reason why the United States has galloped ahead of the countries of Western Europe, in spite of their head start.

There can be little doubt that high labour costs have compelled

* Cf. Neil W. Chamberlain, *Labor*, McGraw-Hill, 1958, Ch. 15; and Seymour Melman, *Dynamic Factors in Industrial Productivity*, Blackwell, 1956.

American employers to use labour far more carefully and efficiently than employers in countries where wages were low. This argument is not, however, as easy to accept as it might appear. Relative costs are rarely, if ever, the result of merely one factor: had the United States been as dependent on overseas trade as some countries, it is certain that American wages would not have risen quite so high without causing adverse repercussions. If countries with a substantial balance-of-payments problem were simply to put wages up to the American level, what would happen would be a crisis that would be resolved, in the short run, by a devaluation of the currency concerned. This would cancel out the pressure on employers and relieve them of the need to seek more efficient machinery.

Since a balance-of-payments crisis, followed by a devaluation, is likely to be accompanied by a curtailment of imports, it may well be that this factor would make the task of raising productivity even more difficult. Inflation may induce a rapid rate of economic growth where it causes no adverse balance-of-payments problems, but it may also check the growth of production by leading to a waste of resources, bottlenecks, and an economic climate that is not conducive to technological innovation.

As time goes on the American people will become more aware of the cost of strikes for other reasons. One of the most important of these is the product of the argument in favour of union militancy. When the capital-to-labour ratio is low, the loss from idle resources is relatively limited compared to the loss that is incurred when the ratio is high. Thus, as industry becomes more capital-intensive, more automated and interdependent, it will become more vulnerable to strikes. If organised labour does not recognise the changed circumstances and use the strike weapon with far more circumspection, there is bound to be a sharp public reaction against unions and a clamour will arise to have their power to inflict industrial losses curbed. The long and costly steel strike in 1959 produced exactly this response. The President of the AFL-CIO has suggested that a national council should be set up to improve the climate of industrial relations. Mr. Arthur Goldberg, President Kennedy's new Secretary of Labour, is a strong supporter of this idea and is likely to favour measures that will promote greater harmony and fewer strikes.

The limits of union militancy are, therefore, determined by the environment in which the union operates. In the future this is less likely to be favourable to strikes than it has been in the past in the United States. Social, economic, and technical conditions will promote closer unity between employers and unions, and there will therefore be less conflict and more collusion. Indeed, it may be argued convincingly that the fall in strikes in the past few years is due to these very factors more than to anything else.

The growth of personnel management

The spread of collective bargaining, the broader coverage and increasing complexity of contracts, and the changing character of industrial relations from conflict to collusion is closely associated with the development of personnel management. Since under the American system of industrial relations collective contracts are binding and must be observed by everyone concerned, a specialised division that is responsible for ensuring that neither management nor the union acts in breach of its undertaking has become a functional necessity of management. The task of selecting, training, promoting, and servicing the personnel employed in modern enterprise is now recognised almost everywhere in America as one that can only be satisfactorily carried out by experts. Personnel management has become a specialised function and ranks in importance with the other specialised aspects of management, such as production, research, sales, and accounting.*

Since personnel managers are concerned with the problems of employees, they naturally have a much greater understanding of the claims of the unions than line managers who are primarily concerned with other aspects of the enterprise. This fact often puts the personnel manager into a position where, in effect, he exercises something of the role of conciliator between senior management and the unions. This development has tended to reduce the area of conflict and bring the unions and management into closer contact. Unfortunately, the fantastic rate of growth of American plants, a high degree of bureaucratisation on both management and union sides, and an excessive degree of formalisation of relations imposed

* Paul Pigors and C. A. Myers, *Personnel Administration,* McGraw-Hill, 1956.

by the fear that unions and management still have of each other has marred this natural development.

In those cases where unionism is still being fought by employers with bell, book, and candle, personnel management has been employed as an instrument to keep the unions at bay. Anti-union personnel policies have, however, only succeeded by matching or even improving upon the gains scored by workers in enterprises which recognise unions.

Personnel management can never be a substitute for unions, no matter how excellent it might be, since in the last resort it must press the point of view of management. It is probable that in many cases of dispute the issue can be resolved equitably and amicably without resort to bargaining procedures. However, there are many fundamental decisions that must be made which vitally affect the interests of union people and which will inevitably be based upon certain value judgements that are open to challenge. For example, there is no immutable distribution of the product of enterprise between the factors of production. Nor is there any unchangeable law governing the prerogatives of management.

It is because they fear that the strength of the unions in relation to that of management will be weakened that American labour organisations take an extremely critical view of the works councils and joint consultative committees which have been an interesting feature of a great improvement in industrial relations in Europe. It is true that these councils were at one time fostered by employers as a counter-union device, and even today there are firms which refuse to recognise unions but have an established works council in their place. But European unions never had to face the wholesale creation of company-controlled unions as did the legitimate trade unions of America in the 1920s. This difference in experience, which was mainly due to the fact that in Europe collective bargaining was on an industry-wide basis and not, therefore, easily undermined by a company-based organisation, has sharply coloured American trade union attitudes.

Worker participation

The joint consultative committees and works councils which have been set up in European countries are not looked upon as substitutes for *bona fide* unions, but as complementary to them. The theory of industrial relations that is widely held in Europe is that managerial decisions may be divided into two kinds: (1) those that are of direct concern to the unions, since they affect immediate conditions of employment; (2) those that are of indirect concern, that will affect conditions of employment sooner or later, but that are not normally subject to collective bargaining. Wages, hours of work, holidays, and so on are matters which would fall into the first category. General problems of efficiency, safety, welfare, and the future plans of the company would fall into the second category. The first category of issues will normally be the subject of collective agreements, which are mandatory on both parties. Issues in the second category will generally be ones on which the workers and the unions may have a point of view, but it is in an advisory capacity that they express their opinions.

The absence of plant bargaining in Europe is an important reason why many of the issues that are regarded as falling within the scope of joint consultation in Britain are the subject of collective agreement in the United States. Since the agreements negotiated by the unions in Europe relate principally to basic conditions of employment there is much scope for local negotiation, which can conveniently be carried on through a works council or joint committee.

The unions do not take responsibility for decisions arrived at by joint consultative committees and works councils, since these bodies represent all workers in the plant, whether organised or not, and they are generally elected on a non-union basis. However, in practice the unions seeks to ensure that they are well represented. In Britain, for example, every worker has a right to participate in the election of a joint consultative committee in a nationalised industry, but by agreement the unions have obtained the right to reserve nominations to union members only. Of course this problem would not arise if the union shop were as common in Europe as it is in America.

Although joint consultative committees have been established on an advisory basis, in practice they very often prove to be an extension of the collective bargaining process. The notion of management that these committees should, in the main, be a channel of communication through which management discusses its plans and problems with representatives of the workers, from whom, in turn, it learns of the matters which are troubling the employees, is largely academic. In the first place, this idea rests upon the assumption that there will be close relations between the representative and his constituents, but in practice these relations are often far from satisfactory. In the second place, it assumes an ability on the part of shop stewards to discuss issues of vital concern to their fellows in an unprejudiced manner. This is to ask the impossible. A shop steward is elected to promote the interests of the union members and he carries this function into discussions of the joint consultative committee or works council. Thus, in practice, joint consultation has often carried the unions into situations which they would not have entered into on their own account.

Although American unions have taken collective bargaining much further than most European unions, American management appears to be far more determined to maintain its past prerogatives than management in Europe. The suggestion by Walter Reuther that the UAW should be allowed to look at the books practically made American employers go purple in the face and speechless with rage at his impudence. When Reuther, at a later date, offered to trade a price reduction of cars for an adjustment of wage demands, the chorus of denunciation at this monstrous invasion of management's sacred responsibility could only be described as hysterical.

The development of the view that workers ought to be partners in industry to an extent that transcends the traditional notion of their right to engage in collective bargaining now extends over a large part of the free world. In Germany, unions in the steel and coal industry have the right to participate on the board of directors, to nominate the personnel director, and to be represented on the works council. In Sweden, France, Holland, and Britain, *comités d'entreprise* have been developed with official support.

In each case the objective has been to achieve a marriage between the belief that every person employed is a partner in a common enterprise and the equally important belief that the interest of employees is different from that of employers and those who exercise managerial authority on their behalf. Also implied is a modification, if not a rejection, of the traditional capitalist notion that men are moved by dreams of avarice to the exclusion of almost everything else. No one would deny that the cash nexus is a fundamental part of the social mechanism of an industrial society, but we know that it is by no means always the dominating arbiter of events. For their lives to be fruitful, people need other compensations besides those provided by money.

It is the apparent preoccupation with money income to the exclusion of all other factors that makes the image of America an unattractive one to millions of people throughout the world. The picture of American society as one dominated by the sign of the dollar is extremely distorted, even while it is not entirely false. Nobody could fail, after living in the United States for a short time, to be aware of the tremendous fund of altruism, neighbourliness, and activity motivated by nobler inspiration than pure material gain. The difference between the relentless, hard, driving activity of life at work and the slower pace of life at home is, in this respect, marked, and in part this accounts for the demand for a shorter working week.

The challenge before Americans in the future will be to democratise industry by finding ways and means of allowing ordinary workers to exercise a more creative role than they occupy as lever pullers and button pushers. A dramatic reduction in the working week to only four days, or thirty hours spread over five days, will minimise the limitations of the industrial bureaucracy that we know today, but it is only a partial solution to a problem which is essentially one of raising the dignity of man in his capacity as an industrial worker.

The big question is whether this can be done without undermining the ability of management to function efficiently and of the unions to retain both the loyalty of their members and the independent bargaining position that they now enjoy.

Although both management and organised labour in the United States contemptuously dismiss a concept of industrial relations based on the notion of common purpose – because it is a threat to a *status quo* which rests upon a sharp distinction between two sides – it is possible that greater participation of employees in the process of decision-making in areas which vitally affect their interest would improve industrial relations. In the American climate of industry this would have to come about in close collaboration with the representatives of the unions in the plants and it would have to satisfy management that the results justified them making this kind of concession.

That such a situation is possible, even under American conditions, has been demonstrated at the Lapointe Machine Tool Company (and a growing number of other companies) where, under the Scanlon Plan, with the co-operation of the United Steelworkers' Union, a revolution in industrial relations was achieved. The implications of the Scanlon Plan were analysed a number of years ago by Clinton S. Golden and Harold J. Ruttenberg in their well-known book *The Dynamics of Industrial Democracy*. A more recent study by a group of experts has confirmed the dynamic possibilities of Scanlon's ideas.*

The basic theory of the Scanlon Plan is that labour should benefit from labour saved while the company benefits from a more efficient use of its assets. The productivity plan is based on the establishment of a normal labour cost for the plant or unit concerned. Whenever the average labour cost falls below this figure the difference is credited to the workers as a bonus paid monthly.

Ideas and effort that will reduce labour costs are encouraged by shop production committees. These committees are empowered to put any suggestion into effect that does not involve some other department in a substantial outlay of money. At a higher level there is a joint committee of management and labour which decides whether suggestions of a wider significance should be adopted. The basic idea is to interest every employee in the decisions of management by linking decisions with the opportunity to participate in them and to benefit directly from their results.

The Scanlon Plan is not merely an appeal to self-interest as in the case of personal incentive schemes, because everybody benefits from the greater efficiency achieved. It is more than a 'group bonus' scheme since its success calls for actual participation at every stage of activity, in every department, from ideas to the actual production function. It is something more than a profit-sharing scheme, since the reward does not depend on factors that are remote from the wage earners' experience and control. The Scanlon Plan also requires active union co-operation to be effective. It is necessary to have vigorous and interested representation and no conflict with other objectives; these can best be achieved through union representation.

* Frederick G. Lesieur (ed.), *The Scanlon Plan – A Frontier in Labour-Management Co-operation*, Technology Press, Massachusetts Institute of Technology and John Wiley & Sons, 1958.

Under the Plan ordinary wage scales and conditions of employment will be bargained in the usual way; this is the basis from which labour cost calculations start. When changes in wage rates occur cost calculations are adjusted accordingly. Finally the Plan does not divest management of responsibility; it reserves the right to accept or reject any idea put forward. In practice, however, the experience of American firms using this plan indicates that more than ninety per cent of suggestions made are accepted.

The acceptance of radical changes is always slow at first, since considerable resistance has to be overcome. However, the growing centralisation of collective bargaining, the increasing complexity of industrial technology, and the social need to find a compensation for trends that tend to make the individual at work a man who has lost his dignity as a human being, will push management and workers into finding a solution that will permit creative participation in the running of industry. We know from experience in Britain, America, and the Soviet Union that an autocratic system of industrial management will produce impressive results from the point of view of productivity. Industrial dictatorship has gradually been modified in the democracies by the growth of the unions, but the fundamental basis of industrial management is still totalitarian in design. The Soviet Union makes considerable play with its so-called system of industrial democracy, which in practice is a more ruthless system of industrial management than capitalist employers have ever dared to impose. The Soviet economy has grown tremendously and though it has yet a good way to go it may eventually catch up with the West in terms of industrial output,* but there is one challenge that the Russians cannot meet, without abandoning totalitarianism, and that is the challenge of democracy. The demonstration of a working system of industrial democracy by the United States would be a powerful attraction to all those who find the authoritarian aspects of Soviet communism and of private capitalism repugnant to their ideals.

Trade unions and profit sharing

A suggestion which evoked a sharp reaction from management as another example of the determination of radical unionists to invade

---

* Gregory Grossman, 'Communism in a Hurry: The "Time Factor" in Soviet Economics'. *Problems of Communism*, May-June, 1959; Colin Clark, *Growthmanship*, Hobart Paper 10, I.E.A., 1961.

their sacred prerogatives was Reuther's proposal that the hourly paid employees should share in the profits of automobile companies. Profit sharing used to be looked upon by management as a means of strengthening the loyalty of an employee to the firm by tying his economic interest to the profitability of the concern. Many employers still consider profit sharing in this light, and for that reason unions have generally looked upon the idea with disapproval.

Profit sharing has certainly not proved to be the panacea for every industrial discontent that its advocates imagined it would be. A bonus is always welcomed by any worker, but most employees at the lower income levels would prefer to receive it as part of their regular wage, if it is large enough to be significant; if it is not, then it is unlikely to make much difference to their attitudes. The profit, when shared out to wage earners, is usually too small, too remote, and too uncertain to have any important influence on industrial relations, unless it is of the kind that is integrated into the reward for the daily production record, as evolved in the Scanlon Plan.

The aspect of Reuther's proposal that set industry by the ears was the suggestion that profit sharing was something that could be bargained about. The leader of the Automobile Workers' Union has claimed that

'The profit-sharing idea was not a demand; it was a mechanism. In the profit-sharing scheme we're trying to find a rational means by which free labour and free management, sitting at the bargaining table, can attempt to work out in their relationships practical means by which you can equate the competing equities – in workers and stockholders and consumers.'

It is likely over the course of time that more will be heard of schemes of this kind, since the question of equity in the distribution of the product of industry is likely to become more of an issue of deliberate decision as the units of production become more integrated and price competition diminishes.

Union control over industrial investment

It has been suggested that American unions might reach a position in which they exercise a powerful control of industrial development through their control of the huge pension funds that now exist in many industries. The implications of the power that the investment of gigantic accumulations of capital could bestow upon the unions were suddenly revealed when the Teamsters' Union decided to use its holding of Montgomery Ward stock to support the incumbent management in a proxy fight.

In most cases the unions have pursued a cautious policy of investing; they have behaved exactly like any other trustee. Where pension funds are jointly managed by representatives of unions and management, the unions have generally been willing to leave the function of managing the funds to professional investment brokers employed by management. There have been indications, however, that some union leaders, notably Walter Reuther, have seen in the growth of pension funds a tremendous opportunity to influence the behaviour of industry and the flow of funds for investment.

There can be little doubt if the control of pension funds were under the aegis of some central agency that their magnitude would be sufficient to give whoever controlled them an exceedingly influential voice in industrial financing. Such a development is hardly likely, and it is improbable that the unions would use their present influence over the flow of pension funds to pursue a social purpose that would be contrary to the normal expectations of their members. If there are developments in the future that give the unions control over the flow of funds to a degree which would permit them in effect to exercise a complete domination over important sections of industry, it is certain that Congress would legislate in the public interest to regulate the power of the unions.

A national council for industry

Industrial democracy will not flourish in an alien environment. It has already been suggested that, for reasons of economic stability, there will have to be closer relations between the unions, employers and government. It would also enhance the prospect of improved industrial relations if there were established in America some organisation similar to the Foundation of Labour, in Holland, or the National Joint Advisory Councils to the Ministry of Labour and to industry which exist in Britain.

These bodies, though only advisory in character, have played an important part in maintaining a healthy industrial atmosphere. They provide an opportunity for the leaders of the unions, industry, and the government to discuss in private the major problems that are likely to have an adverse effect on industrial relations.

Under a Democratic president, as suggested earlier, there is likely to be a growing demand for the establishment of some body of this kind.

It would seem, therefore, that there is a possibility of development along these lines. If this does occur, it will be one more factor in the apparent trend towards a form of social organisation in the United States that is very different from the picture of an individualist, *laissez-faire* economy, which many Americans are so fond of projecting at home and abroad as the image of their society.

VII

Unions and Politics

THE 1958 congressional elections were hailed by organised labour as its greatest political victory since 1936. There can be little doubt that, as the Republicans chose to a greater or lesser extent to run against trade unionism, their resounding defeat and the rejection of right-to-work law proposals, in five out of six states, constituted a major victory for organised labour. The election of Senator Kennedy to the office of President in 1960, after he had been endorsed by the AFL-CIO, set the seal on organised labour's political campaign against the Republicans.

The fact that in the 1958 elections the Republicans suffered a severe set-back persuaded Vice-President Nixon that it was politically unwise to follow the call of Texas and Arizona Republicans to base his campaign on anti-unionsm as they had done in 1958. Nevertheless, in spite of a certain distrust of Senator Kennedy among many trade unionists arising out of his and his brother's activities during the congressional committee's investigation of gangster unionism, the majority of trade union voters in the big industrial areas seem to have voted overwhelmingly for the Democratic candidate in 1960.

The fact that the 1958 and 1960 elections were a bitter defeat for the Republicans is not likely to persuade those who control the party, in any but the eastern industrial states, that they must now come to terms with organised labour. Most Republicans would much like to persuade Congress to adopt legislation that would really make effective what was attempted in section 304 of the Taft-Hartley Act, namely to cut off the flow of funds spent by the unions on political activities, but with the tide running against them they have little chance of succeeding in this or the next Congress.

It becomes more and more apparent that the two principal forces in American political organisation are on the one side organised business, and on the other organised labour. This in effect means that the two American parties are coming closer in their basic structure to the British Conservative and Labour parties. There are, of course, many differences, but before considering them it is worth noting other similarities. Both American parties attract a far wider area of support than their most important groups, business and labour. But in this respect so do the two British parties. Moreover, probably one-third of the members of the British trade unions vote Conservative. What is perhaps most important is that the basic difference in political philosophy and party policy in Britain has been narrowed by the great rise in national wealth and the breakdown of the old social structure to the point where on fundamentals the majority of the two parties are largely in agreement. The Labour Party has, in practice, abandoned socialism, and the Conservatives have embraced the welfare state, although neither party likes to admit its conversion and both claim they have not departed from their pristine positions.* The principal differences which now separate Conservatives from Labour are methods and the mystique which overlays the very long-run goals for which both parties allege they are striving.

In all this there is much that is familiar in the American political scene. The most important differences in the politics of the two countries naturally stem from a different historical experience, geography, and population. America is a much more mobile, volatile, and explosive society than long-settled, temperate Britain. Political opinion, like the climate, runs to greater extremes in America; because there has been no deeply entrenched class structure to bind society together, clashes between groups have been more vigorously expressed. Social insecurity breeds intolerance, and conflict in society is more sharply edged.

---

* This development has provoked a violent reaction of a section of the Labour Party which seeks to compel a return to the doctrines of socialism. If the Party is forced by this revolt to embrace ideas that are completely out of harmony with modern needs it will simply wilt and die as did the Independent Labour Party and the American Socialist Party.

The development of political activity

The history of American labour is, by British and most Western European standards, a bloody one. In spite of the fact that trade unionism is almost as old in America as it is in Britain, the battle to achieve status and respectability has been far more bitter, more violent, and has lasted longer than elsewhere. American trade unions were early involved in politics, but their political significance was always destroyed by the frontier, the immigrant, and the absence of a European-type class structure and its ideological by-product, socialism.

When, in reaction to the failures of the Utopian approach to political organisation, Samuel Gompers persuaded the American unions to withdraw from the political arena, he was at once both profoundly right and wrong. He was right in believing that the unions could be built up only on the basis of fostering the vocational interests of their members, that they could not be made viable collective bargaining institutions on the basis of an ideology that was alien to American workers and had little bearing on the structure and dynamics of American political parties. He was wrong in his belief that American unions could, in their political manifestations, occupy a neutral position from which, in fine impartiality, they could 'reward their friends and punish their enemies'.

It was inevitable that American unions would have to seek closer ties with a party that would defend their interests against the political attacks that were bound to be promoted by employers and their associates who feared the growing strength of labour.

The Democratic Party

In theory the American unions still maintain their neutrality, but in practice they throw their weight behind the Democratic Party. They have become a major source of finance for the Democratic Party, and their contribution is likely to grow more important as time goes on. They also provide the most effective groups of political workers at the ward and precinct level, but they are still far from exercising a dominant position in the all-important state machines. This does not mean that the unions are not free to support Republicans, where they are more liberal than Democrats, or that they are able, on every issue, to compel the Democratic Party in Congress to follow their policy.

The most important factor that complicates the relation of the American trade unions to the Democratic Party arises from the power of the Southern conservatives. So long as the South continues to be a one-party area, dominated by ultra-conservatives, it will be a powerful counter-balance to the power of the unions. In this respect, it is interesting to note that both union leaders and Senator Goldwater* have expressed the opinion that American politics would benefit from a realignment of forces. Many competent observers think that it is likely, over the course of time, that such a realignment will take place. If the Southern conservatives were to join the Republican Party, would it not then be reasonable to describe a Democratic Party without the conservative Southern element as a Labour Party? Like the British Labour Party, it would be a party in which organised labour would be a powerful, but not the only, element. Indeed, unless the unions were greatly to expand their membership, labour would still be a minority group. However, labour as an organised group, and a major source of political funds, would clearly exercise a most powerful influence. On the other hand, a Republican Party without its liberals† would be more like a Continental than the British Conservative Party. But the Republicans, like the British Conservatives, would soon have to move towards liberalism† or risk languishing in the political wilderness. There would, of course, still be differences between the British and American parties, but the differences would not be great in their structure, nor in their policy. Both British parties would probably tend to appear somewhat to the traditional left of the American parties, but over time it is possible that they would turn out to be less radical innovators.

Labour and liberals

It has been a familiar article of belief among British socialists and American liberals that the American labour movement was, in its evolution, some fifty years behind the British movement. From this notion it followed that sooner or later the American unions would be compelled to form a Labour Party on the British model. In recent years, even the most ardent American advocates of this

---

* A leading conservative Republican and strong critic of organised labour.
† Liberals and liberalism are used in the American sense to mean individuals holding views that are similar to those of Mr. Grimond rather than those of Mr. Gladstone.

course have blenched and admitted that the prospect of forming a viable Labour Party in the United States was practically non-existent. It is one of the ironies of history, however, that events are leading to a political situation which, from a party and trade union point of view, will be remarkably similar in the two countries – if the British Labour Party fails to survive as a major political force the similarity will be even closer.

British socialists, who, in their smug insularity, have believed that American labour must go the same way as the trade unions went in Britain, will probably turn out to be right for the wrong reasons. The evolution of the political structure of society has not been either in Britain or America, as they believed, a process of transition from capitalism to socialism, with the unions playing the role of front-line troops always pushing the class enemy back. What has happened, in both Britain and America, is that the course of economic and social development has completely changed the character of capitalism and, in so doing, has left socialism as an obsolete alternative. The evolution of the British labour movement has, in fact, turned out to be one which started with *laissez-faire* liberalism, adopted socialism as its creed, only to abandon it in favour of what might best be described as *laissez-faire* collectivism.* Nationalisation has now been dropped as the universal panacea by all but the fanatics, and the Labour Party has accepted that there is a proper function for both private and public enterprise in a free society. In this progress the unions have played a major role, both as a force driving society towards socialism, and as one constantly tending to curb the desire of the Labour Party's ideologists to adopt revolutionary tactics. Far from being an instrument of radical disruption, the unions in Britain have been a true conservative element, moderating the extremes and softening the process of necessary changes. The conservatism of the unions is at present an obstacle to the break the party must make absolute with old-fashioned Marxist socialism if it is to survive, but this nostalgia is not likely to stand for ever in the way of practical advantage.

In the United States the unions have played a role in some respects more radical than that of their British counterparts, in others

* By this I mean uncontrolled trade unionism and unregulated collective bargaining.

less so. What is most significant is that their pressures have been in harmony with social developments which have produced a political situation that is not very different from that which has emerged in Britain. This is not really surprising, since both countries have gone through similar industrial revolutions, have progressed technologically side by side, and have experienced the same economic vicissitudes and the same upheavals of war.

Having close and sympathetic relations with a party because its philosophy and policy are in general harmony with the objectives of the unions does not mean that the trade unions will necessarily become either creatures of the party or that the party should become a creature of the unions. Whilst it is inevitable that unions will always be concerned about political issues – and they will be concerned about them sufficiently to put some of their resources at the disposal of that party which they believe will most foster their interests – they have a different function from a political party, and they must maintain their fundamental independence. This kind of relationship between unions and political parties which has been achieved in Britain is in principle the same as in America, but differs fundamentally from the position of Communist trade unions, which are under complete political control.

Political power

There are people in Britain, and there are many more in America, who feel that the power of the unions is now so great that there is a pressing danger to democracy. This fear is naturally felt most strongly by those who believe that unions are a threat to their power and privilege, and it would be easy to dismiss it as grossly exaggerated. There is, however, a danger to democracy when any group becomes so powerful that it exercises a political influence to the extent that it threatens to crush organised opposition and destroy traditional civil liberties. It is quite clear that the development of trade unionism in none of the Western European countries, or in the United States, has reached this state of political domination. By comparison with the power exercised in the past on the behaviour of governments by business and associated groups, the influence which the unions wield is still below the critical level.

Although the state of affairs feared by right-wing Republicans and high Tories has not made its appearance, it is the duty of the government, the legislature, and the Courts to protect the rights of the individual against violation by collective organisations. There is, therefore, the problem of the extent to which trade unions and business enterprises should be allowed to use their funds and other resources for political purposes that may conflict with the opinions of some members and shareholders.

Campaign funds

The problem was raised in an acute fashion in Britain in 1908, when a member of a union asked the Courts for an injunction to restrain his union from spending its funds on the support of a political party and in promoting candidates for Parliament of whom he disapproved. The Court, undoubtedly fearful of the rapidly growing Labour Party and the threat to the established social system posed by its policy of radical reform, found in favour of the plaintiff. In spite of the fact that unions had played an active role in politics throughout the nineteenth century, the Court held that the legality of union activity stemmed from the Trade Union Act of 1871, which failed to mention political activities in its description of the functions of a union.

The Osborne judgement threatened the existence of the newly established Labour Party, since it cut off the flow of its life blood, the supply of funds from the unions. The decision had two immediate effects: it led to a clamour for the payment of Members of Parliament from public funds, which the Government satisfied soon afterwards. More important, it underlined the crucial significance of the unions to the Liberal Party, which was then in power. Secretly pleased that the Courts had deprived the Labour Party of trade union funds, the Liberals, with whom the unions had been closely associated before the formation of the Labour Party, refused for several years to introduce legislation to restore to the unions the freedom which they had enjoyed before the Osborne decision. This policy had an effect opposite to that intended. It did not lead to the destruction of the Labour Party, but it did encourage support of the more extreme elements in the unions, who were able to make capital out of the refusal of the erstwhile friends of organised labour to remedy what, to most trade unionists, seemed an injustice. Here, it would seem, is an important lesson for those who would bar the unions from engaging in political activities. The result of any such action would almost certainly be to stimulate the unions to much greater industrial militancy. Deprived of the right to participate in politics through support of a party and parliamentary candidates, they would feel compelled to struggle for their objectives by other means, such as demonstrations and strikes. Though unions are wise to remain detached from party commitments the possible repercussions ought to be pondered carefully before any attempt to prohibit the political activities of the unions is seriously contemplated.

In 1913 the Liberal Government was compelled by events to pass an Act to free the unions from the effect of the Osborne judgment. The Government was forced to recognise that the reaction to the prohibition of political activities by trade unions had worked to the great advantage of its political opponents. The 1913 Act, which is today the principal statute regulating the political activities of unions in Britain, permits them to spend money on political activities on the following conditions:

1. Every union wishing to make political expenditures must establish a separate political fund.
2. Approval for this fund must be obtained by a majority of votes in a ballot of all the members.
3. Every member must be given an opportunity to 'contract out' of paying dues to the political fund.
4. No member who 'contracts out' must in any way be discriminated against; he shall be entitled to all rights and privileges under the union constitution except those solely confined to the administration of the political fund.
5. Every union establishing a political fund is compelled to adopt 'model rules' approved by the Registrar.
6. Any member who may have a grievance arising out of the interpretation of the rules of the political fund is entitled to lay this before the Registrar, who, after investigation, has the power to issue a legally binding order, which cannot be appealed against in Court, compelling the union to redress the complaint.

Out of a total of 660 unions, some 129 have established political funds. The proportion of members contracting out varies from almost none in most of the large unions to as much as 60 per cent in, for example, the National Union of Printing, Bookbinding and

Paper Workers. There seem to have been very few cases of abuse, and complaints to the Registrar have been minimal. How many cases of abuse have not been reported we cannot tell.

Control of union expenditure on political activities in the United States dates from the Hatch Act of 1940, which limited the political expenditure of a 'partnership, committee, association, corporation, and any other organisation or group of persons'. The limit fixed by the Act was $5,000 on any one candidate for a federal office, or to a political committee, in a calendar year. This statute had little or no effect on union contributions to the Democratic campaign in the 1940 election. In 1943 Congress went a stage farther when, angered by the behaviour of John L. Lewis, it passed the Smith-Connolly Act over the President's veto. This statute brought unions under the Corrupt Practices Act of 1925, which prohibited political contributions by corporations. The prohibition, however, only applied to election to federal office; it did not apply to primaries or other nominating procedures, or to state and local elections. Moreover, the Act was far from explicit in its definition of illegal expenditures; thus there were substantial loopholes that were quickly seized upon. The Act, in any case, expired six months after the official termination of hostilities. Congress was therefore faced, when the war ended, with the question of introducing some form of permanent legislation to regulate the political expenditures of trade unions.

Section 304 of the Taft-Hartley Act was the response of legislators to the challenge that it was believed the unions presented to the American democratic system. This section of the Labour Management Act of 1947 amends the Federal Corrupt Practices Act of 1925 to make it unlawful for any corporation or labour organisation to make a contribution or expenditure in connexion with any election of Presidential and Vice-Presidential electors, Senators, and Representatives.

This sweeping legislative attempt to eliminate unions from the field of federal politics has not suceeded in achieving the principal intent of its authors. It has made the unions establish separate funds for the purpose of conducting their political activities, but it has not prevented them from raising large sums by voluntary donation. Following test cases, the Courts have held that expenditure made for the primary purpose of informing members through, for example, the union journal or radio station, of the political views of the union's leadership, is not illegal. It has therefore been possible for the unions to get round the limitations imposed by the Taft-Hartley Act.

On the whole, it would seem that the establishment of separate funds for political purposes satisfies the objection to the use of the general funds of the union on political activities. This procedure permits union members who disagree with the political policy of the leaders of their organisation to refrain from contributions to the political funds. It has been suggested that union members are compelled to contribute to political funds whether they like it or not, but there is little evidence to show that abuse of this kind has been widespread.

If it is considered that unions are spending too much on political activities, it would be far better to tackle the problem by way of limiting the amount that may be spent on promoting a candidate's political campaign. This solution would then assure that all candidates were treated alike and none suffered because their campaign funds were heavily supported by either unions or wealthy business men.

There is also no reason why unions and business organisations should not be made to disclose how they spend money on political activities. If these steps were taken the danger would be reduced of elections being decided on the basis of which party has the largest funds, rather than on the merits of its policy.

There will, of course, be those who will not be satisfied by such measures and who will continue to seek to destroy the political power and influence of the unions by any means they can find. Some Americans fail to remember, however, when criticising unions for engaging in politics, that they have had to fight to establish the right to exist, the right to bargain, the right to strike, and the right to participate in the making of laws which vitally affect the economic and social interests of their members. Nor is it without significance that unions in every country play an important part in politics. It is therefore not surprising that American unions have had to abandon their political neutrality. The experience of most democratic countries shows, however, that unions are generally aware of the danger of becoming too closely identified with a political party. They have learned that a strong measure of independence must be maintained if unions are to exercise a responsible role in modern society. Although the American trade union movement has become one of the most influential factors in the make-up of the Democratic Party, it is not likely to lose sight of the fact that its position will be weakened if it allows itself to be drawn so close that it becomes a political prisoner. In this respect the American trade union movement may have something to teach its British counterpart.

VIII

Conclusions

1. America is passing from an individualist to a more corporative form of economic organisation. This does not mean that private enterprise will suddenly disappear, but rather that technological advance is changing the character of American industrial organisation, its social institutions, and their relations with the state.

The society which is emerging is one in which there is a preponderance of white-collar and service employees. American trade unions have now reached a pinnacle of power and achievement. If they are to climb still higher or even remain there without slipping back, they will have to find the key to organising a larger proportion of the clerical, technical, professional, and service workers who now form the largest group of employees.

It is unlikely that this task can be accomplished unless the unions recognise that they must make concessions to the needs of these groups. This may involve a radical departure from present concepts of union organisation. The challenge which faces the American labour movement is at least as great as that which faced it twenty-five years ago, and it promises to be as difficult to meet.

2. The search for union security, the growth of professionalism, the centralisation of power, have each contributed to the demise of democracy in unions everywhere. In some respects, the process has gone farther in America than elsewhere. This has been primarily due to the extent to which unions in the United States are based upon the law, to the greater need to employ paid officials, and to the practice of giving the senior officer of the organisation almost absolute executive authority.

A reduction in the size of union locals, the election of rank-and-file executive councils, the revision of union rules to permit active opposition and encourage contested elections, and the provision of outside appeals boards on the lines of those already established would encourage democracy.

Changes in the law offering protection to union members when their interests are violated by the ignoring of their constitutional rights, and the enforcement of the ethical codes adopted by the AFL-CIO may make an important contribution to the protection of members' interests.

3. Corruption is not merely a problem of the unions; it is a problem of society. That it hardly exists in British and European unions is not so much due to differences in ideology, though this factor cannot be entirely ignored, as to differences in the ethical standards of industrial and political life. There is a latent hostility to corruption among the membership of American unions that would respond to effective leadership, but so long as members feel, as they appear to do in the longshore and trucking industries, that honesty does not command respect, nor dishonesty retribution, it will not be easy to break away from corrupt practices.

The changes in the law made in the Labour Management Reporting and Disclosure Act put into practice and rigidly enforced, with the active support of the AFL-CIO, may well make a significant contribution towards the achievement of clean unionism.

4. Collective bargaining is becoming more centralised. Under conditions of full employment and a high level of economic growth an inflationary rate of wage increase is difficult to avoid. The essential choice is between controlling the level of demand by monetary and fiscal policy, allowing unemployment from time to time to rise above four per cent, and the establishment of a system of wage and price controls. If controls over wages were adopted, this would not prevent an inflationary rise in prices if, at the same time, the level of demand were allowed to get out of control. Experience in other countries demonstrates that inflation cannot be prevented by a national wage policy alone, although in conjunction with a non-inflationary monetary and fiscal policy a wage

policy might make possible the achievement of stable prices at a lower average level of unemployment.

The political and social pressures which are likely to be exerted in favour of inflationary policies may give rise to another attempt to curb price increases by measures of control over collective bargaining. Success will depend upon an understanding of the basic economic factors involved and the willingness of unions and employers to participate genuinely in making the experiment work.

5. In spite of a highly developed system of collective bargaining strike losses are higher in America than in Britain, but there are fewer unofficial strikes. As major stoppages grow increasingly costly it is possible that further attempts to prevent strikes by legal prohibitions will be made if industrial relations do not improve.

The European system of joint consultative committees is not likely to develop in the context of industrial relations in America. But it is likely that there will be developments towards giving the worker a greater opportunity to participate in the key decisions of industrial management. One way of doing this effectively would be to extend the Scanlon Plan to a much larger number of firms. Unions may also seek greater influence over the distribution of profits and the relative shares of the product of industry.

The importance of securing closer relations has led President Kennedy to establish a new joint union-management organisation in the shape of a national council for industrial and economic problems. A step of this kind has brought the United States into line with many European countries that have such bodies. It is also in harmony with the trends in force in the United States that are inexorably leading to the government playing a more positive role in economic affairs.

If the trends towards a more corporate, centralised and regulated economy were to go too far there would be a danger that the dynamic character of American life might be seriously damaged. Fortunately for the United States there is a strong tradition against trusts, price collusion and monopolies of all kinds which is likely to provoke opposition and counteraction against this trend. In this respect the United States is in a happier position than Britain, where the readiness to press for measures that will stimulate competition is tempered by a widespread preference for the comfortable rather than the competitive way of life.

6. The trade unions are likely to play a bigger political role in the future than they have done in the past. They will almost certainly become much more influential within the Democratic Party, but they will maintain sufficient independence to put their own interests first. If attempts are made to prevent the unions from spending funds on political activities, it is certain in the present climate that they would fail.

Short Bibliography

BRITAIN

Wages

H.M.S.O. Time Rates of Wages and Hours of Labour

H.M.S.O. Reports of Council on Prices, Productivity and Incomes

B. C. Roberts. National Wages Policy in War and Peace

D. J. Robertson. Factory Wage Structures and National Agreements

B. Wootton. The Social Foundations of Wage Policy

Scottish Journal of Political Economy, June 1958 – Symposium on Wages Policy

Industrial Relations

E. H. Phelps Brown. The Growth of Industrial Relations

H. A. Clegg and A. Flanders. The System of Industrial Relations in Great Britain

B. C. Roberts (Ed.). Industrial Relations: Contemporary Problems and Perspectives

Ian G. Sharp. Industrial Conciliation and Arbitration in Great Britain

G. Cyriax and R. Oakeshott. The Bargainers

M. Shanks. The Stagnant Society

H.M.S.O. Industrial Relations Handbook

Industrial and Labour Law

N. A. Citrine. Trade Union Law

C. Grunfeld. Trade Unions and the Individual.

M. Ginsberg (Ed.). Law and Opinion in the 20th Century

A. Seldon (Ed.). Agenda for a Free Society: Sir Henry Slesser, 'The Legal Status of Trade Unions', and J. A. Lincoln, 'Human Rights in Industry'.

Trade Unionism

G. D. H. Cole. Short History of the British Working Class Movement, 1789–1947.

S. and B. Webb. The History of Trade Unionism

B. C. Roberts. The Trades Union Congress, 1868–1921

B. C. Roberts. Trade Union Government and Administration in Great Britain

E. L. Wigham. Trade Unions

E. L. Wigham. What is Wrong with the Trade Unions?

W. Galenson (Ed.). Comparative Labour Movements

T.U.C. Annual Reports

I.L.O. International Labour Review

C. W. Jenks. The International Protection of Trade Union Freedom

U.S.A.

Wages

J. T. Dunlop. Wage Determination under Trade Unions

A. M. Ross. Trade Union Wage Policy

G. W. Taylor and F. C. Pierson (Ed.). New Concepts in Wage Determination

L. G. Reynolds and C. Taft. The Evolution of Wage Structure

Report of the American Assembly. Wages, Prices, Profits and Productivity

Industrial Relations

S. H. Slichter, E. Livernash and J. J. Healy. The Impact of Collective Bargaining on Management

Neil W. Chamberlain. Labor

A. M. Ross and P. T. Hartmann. Changing Patterns of Industrial Conflict

Industrial and Labour Law

D. H. Wollett and Benjamin Aaron. Labor Relations and the Law

Trade Unionism

J. Barbash. The Practice of Unionism

D. Hardman and M. Neufeld. The House of Labor

F. R. Dulles. Labor in America

R. A. Lester. As Unions Mature

Index

AFL-CIO ETHICAL CODES, 101, 119–121, 123, 134–136, 144, 156
'no-raiding' pacts, 119, 136–137
powers over affiliated unions, 145-147, 154, 165
relations with Democratic Party, 187–188, 193–195
role in 1960 Presidential election, 185
Agricultural Wages Board, 20
Airline Pilots, 111
Amalgamated Engineering Union, 54, 79
American Bar Association, 149
American Federation of Labour, 103, 104, 118 (see also AFL-CIO)
American Radio Association, 111
Andrew v. National Union of Public Employees, 81
Anti-trust legislation, 118, 159 (see also Sherman Act)
Antonini, Luigi, 126
Arbitration, compulsory, 10, 48
court, 22
grievance, system of in U.S.A., 171–173
workshop, 52

BAKERY AND CONFECTIONERY WORKERS' UNION, 130, 146–147
Balance of payments, problem of, 64, 161, 174
Ballot, compulsory, 48
Bank rate, use of, 24
Bevin, Ernest, 60
'Bigness' in unionism, trend to, 121–123
Birch, Alan, 63
Boilermakers' Union, 65
Bonsor Case, The, 86

Bossism, 130
Breakaway unions, 82
Bridlington Agreement, 80
Briggs Motor Bodies, 54, 73
British Employers' Confederation, 22, 28
British Productivity Council, 43, 60
Burke, Edmund, 153

CAPITAL RATIO, 34
Catering Wages Boards, 20
Chandos, Lord, 29
Churchill, Winston S., 84, 120
Citrine, Walter, 60
Clayton Act, 105
'Closed shop', see Compulsory unionism
Collective agreements as legal contracts, 35, 55, 122, 158, 170–171, 175
Collective bargaining, 20, 79, 114, 116, 139–141, 157, 161, 178
and inflation, 101
character of, 33, 122
effect of anti-trust laws on, 105
local, 112, 131
Collectivism, laissez-faire, 64, 189
Comités d'entreprise, 178
Common Market, 19
Communication Workers of America, 111
Communist Party, 69, 70, 74, 155
Compulsory unionism, 84, 85, 139–141
outlawing of in America, 107, 138 (see also Taft-Hartley Act)
Conditions of Employment and National Arbitration Order, 82
Congress of Industrial Organisations, 119 (see also AFL-CIO)
Conservative Party, 188

Conspiracy and Protection of Property Act, 44
Conspiracy, doctrine of, 102
Consultation, joint, and joint consultative committees, 56, 176-178
Contract, collective, 51
'sweetheart', 144
Co-partnership, 39
Copeman, George, 39
Corruption, absence of in British and Continental unions, 73, 152
in American unions, 101, 125, 130, 135-136, 143-156
Corrupt Practices Act, 193
Cousins, Frank, 47, 61
Craft unions and unionism, 107, 114, 117
Cripps, Stafford, 27, 63
Crofter Hand Woven Harris Tweed Co. v. Veitch, 85

DEMARCATION DISPUTES, 84
Democratic Party, union support of, 101-102, 185, 187-188
Denning, Lord Justice, 133
Depreciation allowances, 43
Differentials, narrowing of, 109
structure of, 22, 32
Dynamics of Industrial Democracy, The, 180

EARNINGS STATISTICS, 32
Economic growth, rate of, 24
Economic Planning Board, 28
Electoral malpractices, Australian legislation on, 71-73
Electrical, Radio and Machine Workers, International Union of, 110
Electrical Trades Union, 65, 70, 74-75, 79, 118
Employees shareholding, 39

FAIR TRADE PRACTICES ACT, 159
Federal Reserve Board, 164
Ford, Henry, 138
Foundation of Labour, 183
Fraudulent manipulation of union elections, 73, 118
Freedom of association, principle of, 139
Friendly Societies, Registrar of, 67, 73, 87, 192
annual report of, 91
Fringe benefits, 34, 40

GAITSKELL, Hugh, 63
Gas Stokers' Union, 39
General and Municipal Workers, National Union of, 79
Goldberg, Arthur, 156, 174
Golden, Clinton S., 180
Goldwater, Senator Barry, 188
Gompers, Samuel, 103, 152, 153, 187
Gould, Jay, 138
Grand National Consolidated Trade Union, 121
Green, William, 145
Guaranteed wage, 36

HATCH ACT, 193
Hoffa, James, 125, 144, 147, 150, 153, 156

IMPROPER ACTIVITIES IN THE LABOUR OR MANAGEMENT FIELD, Senate Committee on, 100-101, 131, 147
Industrial Court Issues Procedure, 21
Industrial Disputes Order, 82
Tribunal, 48
Industrial unions and unionism, 78-79, 111, 115
theory of, 113
Inflation, and balance of payments, 25, 161
cost-push, 27
problems of 10, 23, 26, 40, 64, 101, 160-161, 165
and productivity, 30, 159
v. depression, 164
wage-price, 24, 50, 160
Inns of Court Conservative and Unionist Society, 17, 87
International Labour Organisation, 60
International Ladies Garment Workers' Union, 126
International Longshoremen's Association, 146, 147
International Typographical Union, 124
Investment policy of unions, 90-91, 183

JURISDICTIONAL STRUGGLES BETWEEN UNIONS, 117-119

KASSALOW, Everett M., 111
Kefauver Committee, Report of, 149

Kennedy, Senator, election as President of, 120, 161, 185
  Bill to eliminate corrupt practices, 150
'Kickbacks', 144, 150
Knights of Labour, 121

'LABOUR', 43
Labour and Public Welfare, Senate Committee on, 143
Labour Management Act, see Taft-Hartley Act
Labour Management Reporting and Disclosure Act, 72, 101, 123, 128–129, 131, 148, 154–156
  powers of Secretary of Labour under, 129, 131, 156
Labour, Minister of, role of, 49, 73
  Ministry of, 32, 50, 52
Labour, movement of, 19, 38
Labour, National Council of, 62
Labour Party, 37, 38, 59, 188–190, 191
Labour Statistics, U.S. Bureau of, 33
Laissez-faire collectivism, 17
Lapointe Machine Tool Co., 180
Legal restraint, freedom from, 16
Lewis, John L., 115, 193
Liberal Party, 66, 191–192
Livesy, Sir George, 39
London Transport, 32

MANAGEMENT, education of, 43
Manufacturers, National Association of (U.S.A.), 150
McClellan Committee, 154
Meany, George, 145–146
Merit awards, 34
Mineworkers, National Union of, 48, 65
Mobility of labour, 38
Monopoly, antagonism to, 157
  fear of, 118
Montgomery Ward, 183

NATIONAL ADVISORY COUNCIL TO THE MINISTRY OF LABOUR, 60, 183
National Amalgamated Stevedores' and Dockers' Society, 81
National Arbitration Tribunal, 165
Nationalisation, 40
National Coal Board, 65
National Health Service, 35
National insurance, 35

National Joint Advisory Council on Industry, 28, 60, 183
National Labour Relations Act, 104, 106, 136, 151
  Board, 84, 106, 136
National Superannuation, 37
National wages policy, 22, 25, 26
Negotiating machinery, 20
New Deal, 104, 106

OPERATING ENGINEERS, International Union of, 147
Osborne Judgement, The, 191-192

PARKINSON'S LAW, 108
Payroll tax, 43
Pension schemes, 37
  finance and investment of, 38
Personnel management, development of, 175–176
Picketing, 53
Police Act, 84
Political levy, 66
Positive Employment Policies, 52
Post Office Workers, Union of, 70
Price stability, 31
Printing, Bookbinding and Paper Workers, National Union of, 192
Profit-sharing, 39, 182
Profits, undistributed, 40
Productivity factor, 30, 43
Productivity, of labour, 173
  rises in, 159, 162
Public ownership, 18

RAILWAY LABOUR ACT, 151
Railwaymen, National Union of, and development of industrial unionism, 114–115
Republican Party, 185–186, 187–188
Resale price maintenance, abolition of, 28
Restrictive practices, 42
Reuther, Walter, 30, 38, 74, 89, 135, 145, 150, 153, 178, 182
Revolutionary syndicalism, doctrine of, 79
Right-to-work laws, 139–141, 185
Roosevelt, President, and the New Deal, 104
Ruttenberg, Harold J., 180

SCANLON PLAN, 180, 182
Shawcross, Sir Hartley, 45
Sherman anti-trust Act, 104
Shop stewards, 11, 54, 56, 178
  Communist element among, 36

Slichter, Sumner, 160
Smith-Connolly Act, 193
South Metropolitan Gas Co., 39
Statistics of earnings, 32
Strike ballots, compulsory, 10
Strike, General, 45, 60
London bus, 23, 50, 61, 90
right to, 44
sympathetic, 44
Strikes, days lost through, 45–47, 168–169
'quickie', 171
'wildcat', 51, 171
Superannuation, 37
Surtax, 43

TAFT-HARTLEY ACT, 44, 49, 106, 136, 138, 141, 185, 193–194
Tariff reductions, 28
Teamsters' Union, 116, 120, 135–136, 144, 146, 151, 183
Terrington Committee, 83
Thomson, D. C., Ltd., 84
Trade Disputes and Trade Unions Act, 44, 45
Trade Union Act 1913, 67, 192
1871, 119
Trade Union Affairs, 147
Trade union membership, 76
Trades Union Congress, 22, 38, 45, 59, 79
authority over unions, 74, 145
co-operation with employers and government, 28
Disputes Committee, 80, 81, 117
Economic Committee, 63
establishment of central appeals committee, 74

and E.T.U. case, 74–75
General Council, 59
on monetary measures, 24
Production Department, 43
and productivity, 40, 43
Report on Structure and Closer Unity, 83
Transport and General Workers' Union, 55, 71, 79, 81, 90

UNEMPLOYMENT, compensation, 36
level of, 163, 167
structural, 31
Upholsterers' Union, 133
United Automobile Workers' Union, 30, 116, 133, 135–136, 159, 172, 182
United Mineworkers' Union, 104
United Textile Workers' Union, 147

WAGE 'DRIFT', 21, 166
Wage, guaranteed, 36
increases and productivity, 159
—price spiral, 24, 50, 160
restraint, appeals for, 27
Wage Stabilisation Board, 166–167
Wages, control of, 26
policy, national, 63
Wages Councils, 20
Wagner Act, 136
Wall Street crash, 104
Webbs, The, 79, 109, 130
Whitley Committee, 56
Wilson, Harold, 63
Winn, Mr. Justice, 74
Works councils, 176–178
Wynn-Parry, Mr. Justice, 81